DOUBLE DOWN

CURRENCY
NEW YORK

DOUBLE DOWN

Bet on Yourself AND
Succeed on Your Terms

ANTOINETTE M. CLARKE
AND TRICIA CLARKE-STONE

Published in the United States by Currency, an imprint of Random House,
a division of Penguin Random House LLC, New York.
currencybooks.com

CURRENCY and its colophon are trademarks of Penguin Random House LLC.

Currency books are available at special discounts for bulk purchases for sales
promotions or corporate use. Special editions, including personalized covers,
excerpts of existing books, or books with corporate logos, can be created in large
quantities for special needs. For more information, contact Premium Sales at
(212) 572-2232 or e-mail specialmarkets@penguinrandomhouse.com.

Library of Congress Cataloging-in-Publication Data
Names: Clarke, Antoinette M., author. | Clarke-Stone, Tricia, author.
Title: Double down : bet on yourself and succeed on your terms / Antoinette M.
Clarke and Tricia Clarke-Stone.
Description: First edition. | New York : Currency, [2019] | Includes index.
Identifiers: LCCN 2018056050 | ISBN 9780525574934
Subjects: LCSH: Women--Vocational guidance. | African American women. |
Women executives. | Career development. | Success in business.
Classification: LCC HF5382.6 .C53 2019 | DDC 658.4/09082--dc23
LC record available at https://lccn.loc.gov/2018056050

ISBN 978-0-525-57493-4
Ebook ISBN 978-0-525-57494-1

Printed in Canada

Book design by Andrea Lau

9 8 7 6 5 4 3 2 1

First Edition

For Grandma, the OG Boss Lady,
who taught us to love big and hustle hard,
whose faith in us inspired us to become
our best and most unique selves

CONTENTS

DOUBLE
DOWN

introduction

Welcome to the New American Hustle

Let's Get It Started

There are two types of people in this world. There's the kind who see power in another person and seek to negate it. And there's the kind who see power in themselves and seek to nurture it. You are the second kind of person.

You bought this book because you're ready to become the person you know you can be. You're ready to become successful on your terms and to be rewarded for who you are, not held back for who you're not. You're done taking advice from people who don't have your best interests at heart. You're sick and tired of being told to wait your turn, pay your dues, follow the rules. You bought this book because you're ready to bet on yourself—and surround yourself with people you will bet on, too.

Because once you nurture the power that's in yourself, you'll go on to nurture the power in others.

Ever since we were little girls growing up in a single-parent household in Ditmas Park, Brooklyn, Mom holding it down like a G, we've pushed each other to be successful on our own terms, offering unconditional support, straight talk, and passionate inspiration. That's how we got to where we are today. And that's what we want to share with you.

As African American women, we've learned a thing or two about owning and operating our confidence, dealing with adversity, and going high when they go low.

As identical twins, we know the power of a partner in crime who always has your back as well as the absolute necessity to individuate.

As first-generation Americans—our parents came here from Jamaica in their teens—we grew up with that better-yourself mentality that all children of immigrants possess.

Refining what we've learned from these experiences and more, we've helped hundreds of women identify their goals, trust their instincts and core passions, and go all-in on their superpowers. Now we want to do the same for you. We're gonna give you all the tools, tricks, and tactics we've learned over the years to help you unlock your best self. We want to help you hustle harder, shine brighter, soar higher, and bank more. It doesn't matter whether you're kicking ass and taking names as an entrepreneur, making a midcareer switch, or just starting out at the bottom of the corporate ladder: you have the power to go to the Next Level. The Next Level is being a Boss Lady in whatever hustle you're running.

What exactly *is* a Boss Lady? Everyone knows at least one or two Boss Ladies. Boss Ladies are found in all professions, in all pursuits, in all things. Because Boss Ladies transcend all professions, all pursuits, all things. *Boss Lady* is a mode of being—an essence, irreducible, elemental. Boss Ladies inspire us. Support us. Believe in us. Trust us. They make us want to be better.

Boss Ladies make decisions, not problems. They *command*, they don't demand. They don't promise, they deliver. They want to make us better, not stay the same. They *answer*, they don't prevaricate. They help us to be our own best selves, not low-res versions of them. They press play, not repeat.

Boss Ladies show grace under pressure, not fear. They act fearless, but they feel fear sometimes. They just know that fear is power—raw. They refine fear into energy, into power. They are power.

And we know that you are one of them. Don't feel like one? By the end of this book, you will.

The Art of the Double Down: Beating the House

Here's the deal. Life is a game of blackjack: again and again you're being dealt a hand of cards, and it's up to you to calculate risk, play out scenarios in your head, know your competition, keep your cool, and play to win. Everyone knows the point of blackjack is to get, well, blackjack, or 21. But wait. That's *not* the point of blackjack. The point of blackjack is to beat the House. That's how you get cash.

See, the odds always favor the House in blackjack. That's how the casinos stay in business. The House has been playing this game for years: it literally wrote the rules. The House calls the shots, it works the odds. The House tries to distract you with free drinks and flashing lights, illusions meant to knock you off your game.

What the House doesn't want you to know is this: you *can* beat it if you play smart and disciplined. Going up against the House isn't easy, but if you want to win, you need to learn how to spot the opportunities where you have a calculable advantage. And then you need to **double down** on it. Doubling down is going all-in when you *know* you have the odds on your side. It's banking hard on the edge you've got.

In life, the **Status Quo** is just like the House. The Status Quo is everywhere. It's all the people and systems trying to hold you back, asking you to settle for less, and giving you second-class rewards for first-class work. It's pernicious. It can even manifest within you as self-doubt and fear, as obstacles to girls, women, and minorities, as a weight that is dragging you down.

The Status Quo wrote the rules, it holds all the cards, and it'll try to knock you off your game in every way it can. It'll try to distract you with false promises and bad role models; it'll try to get inside your head and mess with your heart; it'll convince you that you're always playing catch-up to an ideal that doesn't exist.

The Status Quo is the yin to the Boss Lady's yang: they are locked in an eternal struggle. It's that voice that tells you not to raise your hand or speak up. That voice that says don't bother chasing that opportunity. That voice that tells you not to take the microphone and speak the truth.

That's the Status Quo.

The time you spend worrying whether to wear this or that skirt when you want to be working on your pitch. Acquiescing to your male colleague's request to finish "our work" and e-mail it to him. Thinking that the only way to get ahead is to follow the accepted way of doing things.

That's the Status Quo.

Being forced to choose between "happiness" and "work." Thinking that you can get rich quick if only you get the one right contact or take the right meeting.

That's the Status Quo, too.

The Status Quo is a wily bastard, but all it takes is one winning hand to take him down. That winning hand is you, Boss Lady.

To beat the House, you need to do two things. You need to **double down on you,** and you need to **double down on your crew.** You need to move quickly to get ahead where you spot an opening for yourself, where your passion and your unique skill set will propel you as you blaze a new path forward.

You need to go all-in on yourself—like, yesterday. You need to bet on your unique collection of experiences, passions, desires—the way you *see* and *feel* things—rather than trying to compete with everyone else, on all fronts, in all the same ways. And you need to double down on a solid and loyal crew who'll bet on you, and whom you can bet on, too. Because if you do those two things, you'll be unstoppable. That's what the art of the double down is all about.

Same Same—but Different

Before we start downloading you on how to take over the world, we want to tell you a bit about us. We're Antoinette Clarke and Tricia Clarke-Stone. Best friends. Business partners. Black women. Hustlers. Boss Ladies. And identical twins—or, as *Elle* magazine called us, "Power Twins." As advertising, branding, tech, and media experts, we've helped celebrities, start-ups, household brands, and Fortune 500 companies tell their stories and connect with millions of people. You know it took some hustle to get to where we are today!

Tricia started her career selling radio ad spots for a media company, which meant cold-calling businesses (using a phone book and a landline!) and trying to convince them to advertise on the company's airwaves. Through hard work, creative savvy, and soaking up everything she could learn about the power of storytelling, she is now the CEO and cofounder of the creative and tech agency WP Narrative_. Of the 8,734 CEOs of companies in the media and advertising world, only 93 are black women. Tricia is one of the 93.

Antoinette started out as a production assistant making less than $25,000 a year and working so hard trying to make it in the cutthroat world of TV that she didn't even have the time to go home most nights, opting instead for the one-star not-so-luxury sleep pod she created under her desk. Two Emmy Awards and several career pivots later, she is now vice president of Branded Entertainment and Media Innovation at CBS.

As you'll see from the stories we'll tell throughout this book, we've worked hard—and played hard—to get where we are. And through it all, the Everest highs and ocean-floor lows, we've always been there for each other. When Nette was working those fifteen-hour days as a PA in her twenties making less than $400 a week, Trish helped pay for joint vacations to places like Tulum and Jamaica (we love to travel!). When Trish was going through her divorce in her thirties, Nette stayed up night after night talking her through it (we love to talk!).

Being identical twins was a double-helix twist of fate, and it's made us who we are today. As we like to say, "Same same—but different." On the one hand, we're *so* similar. We look *almost* identical—even some ex-boyfriends couldn't tell us apart! And we sound *almost* identical! Our mannerisms are *almost* identical! We both love Biggie, any Broadway musical, and what we call half-and-half vacations (half-city/half-beach: Havana-Varadero, London-Ibiza). And neither one of us ever met a dress with ruffles or ruching we didn't love.

On the other hand, we are *so* different. We may have the same DNA, but we approach the world very differently. Tricia is a sprinter (fast, targeted, more right-brained), and Antoinette is a long-distance runner (measured, inexhaustible, and more left-brained). Tricia is an entrepreneur (starts businesses to create change), whereas Antoinette is an intrapreneur (steers existing businesses to create change).

We both like change!

We both see new ideas as the backbone of our work, but Tricia has always enjoyed and thrived by assuming risk, looking for new opportunities and rushing to exploit them, while Antoinette prefers the stability of corporate structure, where she can work the levers of power and redefine success from the inside out. We are living proof that there are multiple paths of moving on up in the world. We strongly believe in achieving success on your own terms, not allowing the Status Quo to dictate your dreams or direct your destiny.

Our Promise to You

As high-powered African American women working in mostly white- and male-dominated fields, we've become go-to resources for young women, POC, and ambitious Millennials who, like us, want to be successful on their own terms. They seek us out on Twitter and IG, through LinkedIn and alumni networks. They want to know how they too can be Boss Ladies of their own lives.

The women we mentor are smart and diligent, they've achieved a lot, they plan to achieve more, and they want to make an impact. They don't want to be defined by other people's expectations. They want to create something lasting. They have dreams and they are willing to work for them. They want to know how to break out of the old and into the new. They want to reach the top of their game.

But they're having trouble. They can't seem to figure out the next step, the one that comes after doing everything that's asked of them. They've taken that step, but they haven't moved forward. They're stuck. They're being underutilized but overworked. They want the props they deserve and they want to make a difference, but it's like the Status Quo has stacked the deck, and they just can't seem to get dealt a winning hand.

These women might be like you.

Whether you're twenty-one and hunting for your first "grown-up" job, twenty-eight and wondering why you've been passed over for a promotion, or midcareer and looking to make a pivot, we're guessing that something's off—or standing in your way.

You're passionate, but you're not sure where to place your passion.

You have strong feelings, but you don't know how to channel them.

You know you can make a difference, but you're not sure where.

You believe in your future self, but your faith is being tested.

We get it. We've been there. It took us a while to get to where we're at—and we're still going!—and throughout this book, we're going to share our lessons and stories with you. Because we want you to take what we've learned and improve upon it, because as we progressed in our careers we often found ourselves viewed as anomalies: we were successful women *and* minorities. It was like people were surprised to see us here. We're here to help you take it to the Next Level because we don't want successful women or minorities to be anomalies; we want them to be the norm.

And for us it was the norm. See, we come from a line of strong-willed women—aka the Matriarchy, whom you'll read about later on—and we're all about carrying on that legacy and sense of progress. Mom and her sisters—aka the Aunts—left Jamaica as young women to chase the American Dream. They came, they saw, and they conquered. They made good. They got educated, worked like bosses, and laid down roots. They did it right.

But they also did it their way. And in so doing, they gave *us* the opportunity to do it *our* way. They had their American Dream, and we have ours. That's what the New American Hustle is all about. You don't have to be a doctor, a lawyer, or an engineer to get respect, stability, and props. You don't have to become something that you're not to live large and be celebrated for who you are. And the New

American Dream is about success redefined—success on your terms, not the Status Quo's.

Double Down

Double Down is divided into two parts, since we've always thought there are two important things in life: the brilliance you inspire in yourself, and the brilliance you inspire in and with others.

In **Part One** we'll focus on how to double down on yourself. The first thing you're gonna learn is: all success starts with strength. We'll teach you how to defy outmoded Status Quo thinking, stand out from the crowd, understand and articulate your value, and hone—and own—who you are. We'll teach you how to use all your knowledge when moving into new career spaces—even, and by that we mean especially, the risky ones. And we'll talk about the importance of focusing on the Long Game: always keeping your eyes on the horizon, while moving forward with purpose and a plan of action.

Once you've started the ongoing process of unlocking your best self, in **Part Two** we'll help you look outside yourself. That's where your Crew comes in. This is about strategically surrounding yourself with people who are ready to double down on you. We'll talk about how to curate and activate your Crew with nuance and care, rather than what the Status Quo would have you do: accumulate relationships passively and then let them gather dust. We'll talk about the importance of having an Ace riding shotgun: someone who will check your blind spots, help you navigate the terrain, and have your back at all times. We are living proof that there's nothing better than having a partner in crime! And we'll teach you how to get in front of the people who matter, demonstrate your worth without overplaying your hand, find gurus (and lots of them!), and understand the power of alliances to further your career.

If you're a true Boss Lady, and we know you are, then you gotta be a leader, and you'll learn how in the last chapter. But we aren't talking about your job title. We're talking about instilling confidence in your people, being fearless in the face of adversity, and showing up as a Boss Lady who's ready to run the world. Yeah, you read that right. Run the world.

Throughout *Double Down,* we'll interlace our own stories (about growing up in the Matriarchy, our early side hustles, and how we got to the tops of our professions) with inspiring tales of the Boss Ladies we admire most. You'll meet OGs like Anne Wojcicki, the founder of 23andMe; Loren Ridinger, the cofounder of Market America and founder of Shop.com; Carly Cushnie, the founder of Cushnie; Grace Mahary, model and philanthropist; Ayesha Curry, entrepreneur and TV personality; Lacy Phillips, Manifestation Advisor and founder of To Be Magnetic; Ali Kriegsman and Alana Branston, founders of Bulletin; Tyra Banks, supermodel and media power player; Lena Waithe, the first black woman to win an Emmy Award for Best Comedy Writing; Tori Bowie, one of the fastest women in the world and Olympic gold medalist; and many more. And at the end of each chapter you'll find a section called **On the Download,** where we'll distill the core principles we want you to remember. We suggest writing them down in your journal; reading them will give you strength during the trying times. There are fifty-two of them, one for each card in the deck. Play them wisely; play them to win.

Make no mistake: it's tough out there. The game of life, like blackjack, isn't for the faint of heart, the weak of will, or the lacking in love. The House is still stacking the odds by keeping women and minorities down. Sure, progress is being made. But women still make seventy-eight cents for every dollar a man makes. Women are still less likely to be promoted even when they're as qualified as their male peers, and only 6 percent of Fortune 500 CEOs are women. Boss Ladies: it's time to change all that.

We can't tell you how many times we've been told to "wait our turn" or told that things weren't done "that way." We know that you, too, have heard things like this.

We know your passion isn't being properly utilized by those in power.

We know you have ideas that could change the world.

Enough is enough. It's time to stand up and stand out. As Bey says, "Power's not given to you. You have to take it."

We wrote this book to help you take the power back. We wrote this book for you. It's an invitation. We want you to be the next Boss Lady to join our crew.

So, what are you waiting for?

Let's get started.

Antonette & Tricia

On the Download

The Status Quo

The get-in-line, wait-your-turn, pay-your-dues, you-can't-do-that mentality that governs most of the world and manifests inside your head as self-doubt and fear. This is what you're up against.

Boss Lady

The confident, cool, and compassionate leader who remains a fearless optimist in the face of relentless Status Quo pressure, as she kicks ass and takes names. This is what you are.

Double Down

The action of surveying your creative or professional terrain, seeing an opening where you know you have a calculable advantage, and seizing the opportunity. This is how you'll succeed. Go all-in.

New American Hustle

The journey of refusing to follow the traditional script or play the Status Quo parts, opting instead to be the author of your own destiny by redefining success on your own terms. This is the Long Game you're playing.

part one

DOUBLE DOWN ON YOU

chapter one

Don't Emulate, Originate

Our mom is a Swiss Army knife.

Mom was born the youngest of eight brothers and sisters in May Pen, Clarendon, a small Jamaican town with narrow, winding roads that used to overflow with brown people going to and from the marketplace, baskets in their hands or on their heads. In the evenings, Mom's mom, Grandma, liked to host the neighbors at her home, dragging a TV onto the veranda after the sun slipped below the sea so everyone could gather around to watch. Family and friends sat in the yard, drinking island drinks like milo, sorrel, or Wray and Nephew. Grandma knew how to throw a party. She was the Matriarch of the Bryan Clan, a Caribbean Queen. She was dope AF.

Mom wanted to get the one thing that no one can take away from you—education—so in 1972, when she was seventeen, she immigrated to Brooklyn to chase the American Dream. By then her brothers, our uncles, were already in engineering school in the States; one sister, Norma, was in nursing school in Scotland, while Monica had just completed her education and was working and living in Brooklyn with Leonie. Our family is *obsessed* with education.

Mom wanted to be a nurse, so she studied biology. She loved the complexity of invisible processes at work. But after two years of school, she got pregnant by our father, whom she'd been dating since before she left Jamaica. Grandma and the Aunts thought Mom was throwing away her future by having a child at such a young age—and out of wedlock! They were furious. They worried she was going to drop out and become a stereotype: a poorly educated, unmarried immigrant who didn't make any money—with a kid!

Correction: kids! That's when we entered the picture—March 18, 1976, at 1:00 a.m. and at 1:05 a.m. at Downstate Medical Center in Brooklyn. At four pounds each, together we were about the weight of an average baby girl. Mom was in labor for twenty hours, and Dad was there to greet us on our way out. Our parents married soon after, but it only lasted a few years. When we were four our dad got abusive, and Mom did what she needed to do to protect herself and her daughters. The divorce, while necessary, left us feeling *vulnerable* and sad.

When Dad left it was like we lost a piece of our family puzzle, and then we started to feel like he saw us less as his children than as a possession over which he shared custody with Mom. Our dad's mother and the rest of his folks started to treat us differently after the divorce: they blamed Mom for not trying to work it out, and we became a proxy for her. After a few visits to our dad's mother that left us reduced to tears in the bathroom because we felt so iced out of their family's love, we realized we needed to be around people who gave us support, not trouble. Dad got remarried and became a piece in another family's puzzle. While we saw him and talked on birthdays and holidays—even went on a great cross-country drive with him once when we were teenagers, hitting up diners for breakfast and roadside attractions in the midday sun—we never really knew what it was like to have a father around.

None of this was easy on Mom either. It wasn't like she *wanted* to be single, but she needed to look out for herself—and us. Grandma and the Aunts (Monica, Leonie, and Norma) filled any gaps that were left with our father's departure and served as our village, making sure Mom landed on her feet and that we didn't get lost along the way. We spent every weekend with Grandma at her apartment on Turner Place, not too far from our place in Ditmas Park, Brooklyn, and soon enough we became known to the rest of the family as the Supremes; or Luke, Leia, and Han Solo; or just the Three Stooges. What can we say—we shared Grandma's sense of humor, and we all like to joke around! All the while, Mom hustled her way up the ladder from administrative assistant, to executive assistant, to chief of staff to the president of a large hospital, typically taking on a second job to pay for our Catholic school tuition and dance classes.

She *worked* hard. But she also *played* hard. We learned that from her. She knew how to have fun and she communicated the importance of living it up to feel alive.

Above all else—well, of course, except for us—Mom *loved* music. Mom was like a living mixtape, a breathing playlist, a walking Spotify. When we were little, we woke up every morning to all different types of artists—Pat Benatar, Air Supply, Hall and Oates, Fleetwood Mac, Beres Hammond, Sanchez, Supercat, Chicago, George Michael, Bob Marley, Tina Turner, you name it—blaring on the speakers, making the air around us electric with possibility and joy. Mom bopped to the music while she cleaned the house and cooked up a big pot of oxtail or stew peas. That's how she worked her groove, blasting "Hit Me with Your Best Shot" and "Invincible." She gave us the bug.

So, when we were eight and heard that MJ was coming to town on his "Victory Tour," we told Mom we *had* to go. We wanted to revel in the spectacle—where the music and the energy and the lights and the *feeling* all came together as part of a *total experience*. But the tickets were expensive, and the concert sold out immediately. When we heard, we were crushed.

Mom was not. She knew she'd figure something out. Where there's a will, there's a way—and a Boss Lady.

One day at work, her boss asked her to put in a call to a powerful person to get his kids tickets to that very concert. Mom was like, "I don't want to overstep, but my kids adore Michael Jackson. Can I ask about tickets for them, too?" That was how she rolled: working his clout and connections to get tickets not only for him and his kids but also for the two of us and our cousins Michelle and Tracey, who were like our big sisters. When we got to the concert at the Meadowlands and saw that huge stage and the bright lights and felt the energy of the crowd, we were in awe. It was mind-blowing. We even had good seats! This man we listened to on the radio, on vinyl, on CDs came to life right before our eyes. And he was . . . wait for it . . . moonwalking. *Smooth criminal!* On this day, Tricia became obsessed with MJ, and for years to come a white glove was never far from her hand.

Mom made that magic happen for us. She had a solution for everything. As we said, Mom was a Swiss Army knife.

This was just one of the many times Mom refused to let an obstacle get in her way. From small ones like scoring concert tickets to big ones like providing for two kids as a single parent, Mom faced down every problem from a place of strength. We learned that from her. And that's what we want to teach you, too.

Success Starts with Strength

All success starts with strength. Any obstacle, no matter how significant, can be overcome when you start from your place of strength.

And no obstacle, no matter how *in*significant, can be overcome *unless* you start from your place of strength.

Mom was our strength. She was the first person who gave us the permission to believe we could do anything. She flaunted the rules of the Status Quo. We saw her sacrifice, demonstrate ingenuity, and balance the high-wire act of working hard and living well. She taught us to embrace our femininity, to see being a woman as an asset, not a hindrance. Mom was audacious, she was audacity in heels. She took us on adventures all over the city—to the ballet, to the cosmetics counter at Saks, and to the Public Library. Mom taught us to show empathy while still being "alpha" enough—strong, ambitious—to make our way in a man's world. All the doors in the world were open to us, she said, we just needed to walk through them. Mom helped us see that true strength is believing in yourself—but that just as important is having other people in your corner who believe in you, who believe you can do anything you set out to accomplish.

We also learned to use those different Swiss Army tools we saw her whip out again and again—confidence, compassion, ambition—to solve any problem that came our way, and eventually we added a few tools of our own. And from watching our mom do the impossible—support and nurture us through thick and thin without ever giving up or giving in—we learned that a woman on a mission is a mighty warrior capable of superhuman feats. Mom's essential duality, power paired with sensitivity, the capacity for both feeling and doing—that's where we both derive our superpowers from.

We know that you have someone like Mom in your life, too. Someone who gave you strength and permission to own your uniqueness, who showed you that hard work and persistence pay off. Someone who saw your greatness waiting to bloom and gave it precious nourishment.

Maybe it was your dad, who taught you about history and science and how to change a tire. He taught you that curiosity opened portals into new worlds. "You can grow up to do anything," he said.

Maybe it was the coach who wouldn't let you quit when you were sure you'd pushed yourself to your limits; instead, she showed you that you could push harder. "I've seen the fire in you," she said. "You can *win!*"

Maybe it was the teacher in high school who took you seriously, who saw your talent and encouraged you to use it. "You should write for the school paper. You're the most natural reporter I've ever seen!"

Do you remember how special you felt—how *understood*, how *seen*, how *powerful*?

And again. This is what life should feel like all day, every day, that sense—that you're doing the thing you were put on this planet to do. We want to help you feel this way again. And again. And again. And again.

If you don't feel this way right now, that's okay. We didn't always feel this way either. The world is a fast-moving and confusing place, with many things that can knock you off your game on any given day. We know that when you have a bad day or a bad week, it's easy to fall into an abyss of Chinese food takeout, dirty duvet covers, and low-budget rom-coms. And don't get us started on the obstacles women face in and out of the workplace—from the slights, to the sniping, to the lower pay for the same work. But take it from us: all the BS, all the noise, all the haters—all that stuff melts away like blowtorched butter when you start from your place of strength.

You Gotta Differentiate Before You Originate

We grew up in the 1980s as New York City was going through a tough time—rising income inequality, crime, the AIDS epidemic.

Luckily, we had some isolation from that in sun-strewn Ditmas Park, Brooklyn.

We were each other's best friend, but it wasn't always easy.

Hey Nette, wanna share everything from the ages of one to eighteen with someone five minutes younger than you?

Hey Trish, do you want to have a clone, a person who other people will think is you for all your life?

Asked no one, ever.

When we were growing up, we rarely even heard our own names! It was always *the Twins*. Our plurality became singular. If one of us did or said one thing, the other was expected to parrot it. People saw us as pretty, identical faces to entertain and do tricks, never to say interesting things. It was a lot to deal with, especially since we would've had enough on our plates simply by being girls and black! In retrospect, it probably didn't help that Mom decided to dress us *exactly the same for our entire childhood.*

Once, when we were very little, our uncle was watching us while Mom was out working and he accidentally mixed us up and fed Antoinette twice. When Mom came home and figured out what had happened—Tricia was hungry!—she came up with a bling solution: she got us gold bracelets with our names on them! Having a way to differentiate ourselves ever so slightly felt awesome. We wore them till we were ten—and sometimes still sport them on Throwback Thursdays.

Even though Mom couldn't resist dressing us alike—in her defense, the photos in the albums are damn cute—she saw we had very different personalities and tried to give our natural differences room to grow. She got us into separate classes at our Catholic grade school, Our Lady of Refuge, on Ocean Avenue, and then at Bishop Kearney, an all-girls Catholic school in Bensonhurst. Which meant that from kindergarten to eighth grade we spent the majority of our waking hours like you—as a singleton.

This gave us time to explore our passions separately—and it forced us to locate what made us each special. After all, we'd felt special for the first five years of our lives because we had the other! We'd grown accustomed to the power of the *wow* factor, as in "*Wow*, you two look *exactly* alike" or "*Wow*, how does anyone tell you apart?" We'd gotten used to relying on what we call our Twinity—the special magical power of being a twin—to define us, and we didn't know who we were without it.

Suddenly, we were like, *Wait, where's all the attention we used to get? We were just starting to work a room!* In essence, we had learned to play tennis by playing doubles; now we had to play singles! We had learned how to finish each other's sentences, and now we were feeling like lonely dependent clauses! Essentially, we had two identity crises—(1) *Whoa, we are inseparable!* and (2) *Whoa, we are separable!*— before we learned cursive or our times tables.

With the *wow* factor gone, during the school day, at least, we were suddenly in a great hurry to stand out. And this forced us to work hard to make ourselves as powerful a force as individuals as we were together.

Over time, we cultivated our differences. Antoinette was always more creative and girly, writing intricate stories and poems, making paper cutouts, and planning the next day's outfit. Growing up with severe asthma—seriously, her asthma was *terrible*, and she's still allergic to about ninety-nine things—prevented her from being more active, more adventurous. But that handicap also forced her to learn how to think things through—how to plot and plan. Because her asthma often forced her to be the kid watching from the sidelines, she honed her powers of observation, and over time she became acutely aware of the way people *connect*—and how much we all yearn to have our emotions seen and heard.

Tricia was a tomboy from Day One, announcing that when she grew up she wanted to be a rock star: a life calling that required a new Fender guitar *and* the latest Casio keyboard (to compose her magnum opus, of course). She loved gadgets and was unafraid to try new things. She's riskier and more carefree to this day, keen to move quickly and break things, while Antoinette is often the voice of reason and reflection. From the get-go, Trish always loved to talk and be the center of attention, whereas Nette was shyer, more emotionally inquisitive. And since Antoinette was often sick growing up, Tricia (even though she was five minutes younger) became her protector, ready to sound the alarm if she sensed an asthma attack coming on.

Our process of differentiation was also a process of introspection. We were looking inside ourselves to find what made each of us who we were. We didn't know it at the time, but we were rummaging around in the dark, looking for our superpowers. It took us a long time to find them, but when we really boil it down like kale, Tricia's superpower is *action* and Antoinette's is *empathy*. Tricia is all about *doing*, solving a problem and then moving on to the next. And boy, does Antoinette know how to *feel* for another person, how to identify what people need and want, and then help them get it.

Antoinette came by her superpower the hard way, maybe the only way: she felt a lot! It was in third grade that she discovered how she could put her strengths to work for the first time, when her third-grade English teacher, Mrs. Santoriello, told Antoinette that her stories "came to life on the page." It was the first time Nette had ever thought about her stories in that way—*and it was magical!* Mrs. Santoriello said Antoinette was so good that she should become a journalist when she grew up. That made *sense*. From that day onward, Antoinette was determined to become the next Sue Simmons, who at the time was the only black female news anchor on any of the local New York news stations.

When Antoinette heard her passion and ability articulated in that way by someone "in the know," someone she trusted, it all clicked for her. She thought to herself: *I am good at writing about people. I could do that.* And at that moment, Antoinette knew for the first time that she had a superpower.

Double Down on Your Superpower

Do you know what your superpower is? Let's put it another way: What's the common denominator of all your proudest moments? What consistently sets you apart from your peers? What do you do so effortlessly that it can feel like magic?

At the end of the day, whatever you feel *magical* doing—that's your superpower. It's really quite simple. Superpowers are so obvious we often don't realize we possess them. It's almost as if there's a conspiracy out there to convince us we don't have *any* superpower, let alone the superpower we *do* have.

The reason you doubt your powers is because the Status Quo *wants* you to doubt your powers. Why? Because the Status Quo wants everyone to be the same; it wants everyone to be average, ordinary, rule following. The Status Quo doesn't believe in individuality and it has no use for subtlety. It's not your imagination: there really is a conspiracy to make you feel unspecial. F that!

You *do* have a superpower, and it's time you started celebrating it. But not just celebrating it, exploiting it. You need to double down on what makes you *you*. There are too many well-qualified people in the world who either want your job or have the one you want for you not to start cultivating your unique value right now. Just being as good at all the same stuff that others are—whether that's Photoshopping, pitching clients, telling jokes, or writing copy—will only get you so far. The thing that sets you apart is what will allow you to shine. Understanding, elevating, and playing to your uniqueness is the only way you can stand out from the crowd. By knowing what your strengths are and doubling down on them, you will transmit your worth to the world.

The first time we really doubled down on our superpowers together was when we were twelve years old. Aunt Leonie was working on the Upper West Side near a store called Trocadero that sold many of the top brands at the time. This was back when Guess was starting to get really cool, and Trocadero stocked Guess sweatshirts at a steep discount. Naturally, we each got one—Antoinette's was blue, Tricia's red—and wore them home. That's when we had our idea.

NETTE

Damn, you look *goooooood.*

TRISH

You look pretty damn *goooooood* too. We should throw down on these and sell them to kids at school.

NETTE

Truth!

Since we went to Catholic school and wore uniforms, there were only a few days every month that we were able to wear regular clothes. This was the day to show off your style! We figured we'd premiere our sweatshirts on the next Dress Down Day—and if our people liked what they saw, we'd invest in buying more to sell at a profit! Win-win.

On the next Dress Down Day, Tricia made sure to walk all around school, down one hall and up the next, like a peacock strutting his stuff. Meanwhile, Antoinette casually talked the sweatshirts up to anyone who would listen and sold everyone exactly where they could buy one. It was our one-two punch.

And it worked. Everyone thought the sweatshirts were lit and so we used our saved Christmas money from the past two years to buy ten new ones—and then flipped them. We made $400 in profit!

This was our first taste of entrepreneurial success—and it tasted as sweet as chocolate syrup and felt as smooth as silk! We learned that we could solve problems for people if we had a good idea, saw an opening, and went all in. It started with our believing in our idea and in ourselves.

Tricia worked her adventurous streak and love of action, while Antoinette worked her ability to connect with others and meet them where they're at. This was the first time we really worked together, and it felt like magic. Tricia boldly put the idea out there, while Antoinette told the story around it. It was the first time we truly understood the power we had in this world to turn our passions into opportunities, if only we embraced our superpowers, and doubled down on them.

The Three Cs: Confidence, Cool, Compassion

Just like eyelash extensions or a beautiful lawn, success takes work to maintain. In the same way your passion is pointless if you don't follow it, what's the point of having a superpower if you don't nurture it? The Three Cs are the nourishment superpowers need to thrive.

Mom modeled confidence, cool, and compassion like her life depended on it.

She was just one single little Jamaican immigrant lady (clocks in at 5'2") with a set of tiny twins, but she never treated herself like an outsider or an underdog. She always believed that if you have value and you articulate it to the world, you will be valued *in and by* the world.

That was her confidence.

Mom also did it *her way*. She was no cookie cutter—but she was a tough cookie. Mom cultivated her own personal style, she rocked out to her own eclectic musical soundtrack, and she taught us to do the same.

That was her cool.

In the midst of her own career, Mom never stopped looking out for us or her family. She felt everyone was stronger together. She made sure that we looked out for our people and those who were less fortunate.

That was her compassion.

To make the most out of your powers and start getting acknowledged as the stone-cold Boss Lady that you are, you want to focus on these three key qualities: Confidence, Cool, and Compassion.

CONFIDENCE: BE OPEN TO YOUR OWN AUDACITY

Not everyone who is confident is successful. But you can't be successful without being confident. It's that simple. All Boss Ladies on Planet Earth have confidence. All Boss Ladies believe in themselves. It's a prerequisite.

If you believe you'll succeed, you probably will. If you believe you'll fail, you definitely will.

Read this over and over again because it's one of the truest things in the world and we never want you to forget it:

If you believe you'll succeed, you probably will. If you believe you'll fail, you definitely will.

We aren't suggesting that you can simply envision your success and it will happen. But look at it this way: If you don't have confidence in yourself, how are you going to convince funders to back you, your boss to give you a raise, or your colleague to bring you in on that new project? If you don't know deep down that you have something unique to offer the world, why would the world take notice of you? How are you going to be an artist if you are too self-conscious to share your work? How are you going to start a business if you're too humble to tell your friends, "I'm starting a business"?

In short: **if you don't believe in yourself, you can't expect others to believe in you either.**

No matter what industry or business you're in, being able to kick ass at your job has as much to do with confidence as it does with ability. Some people have no ability but a lot of confidence, and they can go a certain distance on sheer confidence alone. Other people have a ton of ability but zero confidence—and they get nowhere! There's no substitution for hard work and ability, for sure. But you need confidence to get out there and make things happen. You need confidence to get seen. And if you're not seen, you're not going to rise up.

All Boss Ladies have moments of self-doubt. Of course. The Status Quo is relentless in trying to tell us we're not good enough, smart enough, skinny enough, calm enough, kind enough. We receive these messages at every turn, from influencers' manicured Instagram stories to haters telling you to be more like this or more like that. But you'll never be happy pretending to be someone who you are not. That's why we insist you double down on who you actually are.

The beginning of confidence is being open to your own audacity. If you plant the seed, it'll start to grow—a little at first, like a sapling taking root, and then it'll rise up strong and tall.

But you need to nurture it. That means you may need to show to yourself—and later, to others—that you can deliver. You should seek to build confidence in low-stakes arenas so that when you're finally in the mix you can remain calm and chill. And the more confident you become in one area of your life, the easier it becomes to replicate that confidence elsewhere. Because, like a great start-up idea, confidence is scalable.

Buying those Guess sweatshirts when we were fourteen was a risk, our first real risk as entrepreneurs—and we spent virtually all our capital on that first run. But it was a risk we were willing to take because we had confidence in our idea and ability to execute it. We'd done our homework first—though not literally, of course, we hated homework—so the risk didn't feel so scary. We knew that other kids wanted the sweatshirts: We'd created a need, and we rushed to meet it. We were open to our own audacity.

Confidence is essential to risk taking, and risk taking is the name of the game if you're going up against the Status Quo. If you're a woman and you live on Planet Earth, there will always be someone with power who thinks you don't have what it takes to make Big Decisions. There will always be people who try to feed your self-doubt, like fanning flames with O_2 and gasoline. There will always be people who underestimate you, no matter how successful you are. You need to prove those people wrong—and before you do, you need to know that you can and that you will.

Ironically, haters can actually be the biggest confidence boosters there are, because they force us to double down and prove our worth—as much to ourselves as to others. Take Tyra Banks—supermodel, media mogul, and creator of *America's Next Top Model*. Antoinette worked with Tyra for years and learned up close how haters can become fuel for confidence.

"I love being underestimated," Tyra once said. "I love when they think, *Oh, she's just a model, she's going to sit there and do nothing. . . .* When I was a model, my biggest obstacle was that I was black and curvy.

When I went into producing, my biggest obstacle was that I was a model. But, as I say to the girls on *Top Model,* anybody who is at the top of anything has taken risks and withstood criticism and hardship. I say: *You think I'm just a model? Well, then, let me show you."*

Tyra knew she was beautiful, and she doubled down on that unique beauty and put it to work early on in her career. "I made my living being twenty or thirty pounds heavier than the average model," she says. "And that's where I got famous."

But it's often not enough to simply be confident; you also have to let the world know it! When Tricia graduated from Skidmore College in 1998, she landed an interview with Emmis Communications, a big media company that owned a lot of radio stations. Tricia had plenty of experience *listening* to the radio but zero experience relevant to this particular job, which was in ad sales.

She met with the director of sales and a sales manager, both of whom were male, white, and in their midthirties. Tricia was black, female, and twenty-one.

THEM

Why do you think you can do this ad sales
job? You have no experience.

TRICIA

I know I can sell.

THEM

How? What have you done?

TRICIA

I've promoted parties. I've had to convince
proprietors to give me specific nights at
their venues, a risk for them, and I've
learned how to encourage, engage, and entice
people to come to an event and pay for it.

It was a stretch, but they bought it—hook, line, and sinker. Two weeks later, they called her to offer her an entry-level position to be an account manager representing Hot 97, KISS-FM, and CD101.9—some of the nation's largest radio stations.

And that's how Tricia got her start. She went to work as one of the youngest members of the team and one of the few POC. Tricia had the confidence in herself to interview for a job she wasn't technically qualified for, and then she laid out her value-add. Once you begin to be open to your audacity, that's when doors begin to open for you.

COOL: APPLY YOUR CULTURAL INTELLIGENCE LIBERALLY

We don't need to tell you that the Status Quo is *not* cool, but it might surprise you to learn that coolness is one of your best weapons to take it on. Why?

Because everyone *loves* cool and everyone wants *to be* cool. Companies want to be cool, customers want to be cool, clients want to be cool, bosses want to be cool. Cool sells. Cool delivers. Cool is queen.

Cool is cultural intelligence—knowing what's going on. Because culture is who we are—it is the who that dictates what we identify with, what we crave, what will call us to action, and what we ultimately buy into. Cool is taste. Cool is foresight. Cool is authenticity. *Cool is the subversion of the Status Quo with style.* Cool is running as an underdog in a House race against a ten-term incumbent, winning, and becoming the youngest woman ever to serve in Congress. Wepa, AOC!

There are levels to cool.

For your purposes, cool has two applications—for you, and for your work. Knowing what's cool in a professional context is in the DNA of what you do—and not just for those who work in fields like media or fashion or culture. You're already assessing coolness quotients all the time without knowing it—*What can I do that's new? How can I make this project unique? What will really impress people?*

The answer is to find the cool angle in whatever you're doing.

At Tricia's first job, at Emmis Communications, knowing what was cool ended up being what helped her move ahead. From the get-go, she wanted to go *big*! In the beginning, Tricia assumed that the best way to prove her worth was simply by closing lots of sales. So she pored over magazines, studied *Billboard* charts, and took the D train uptown to the Bronx to cold-call small businesses. At the end of her first year in 1999, she'd closed more than $1 million in new business and had more than doubled her $35,000 salary. That's legit!

But when she started asking management for bigger, more established accounts, they told her to wait her turn. They kept saying things like "There's a track you have to follow, you have to pay your dues." Blah, blah, blah . . . You know, Bullshit Status Quo logic. She was making a real impact, but they weren't recognizing it. That's when she realized that even though she was doing very well, it was the same *very well* that everyone else was after. She was good. But Status Quo good.

So, she started thinking, *I can't compete with the level of experience the senior people have, so what do I have that they don't have? What will set me apart?*

She took stock and looked around. Despite having put in a solid year, her colleagues were still treating her like the new kid. But, she realized, they were also treating her like the "cool kid." Because of her youth, she had become the go-to barometer for what was going on culturally, constantly being asked, "Who are you listening to?" "Where's the new hot spot?" "Where did you get that outfit?" They didn't take her work as seriously as she deserved, but they sure did want a part of her cultural relevance and knowledge.

This was at the height of the first dot-com boom, and most of her colleagues had yet to fully grasp the Internet's potential the way she did. Some days, she'd have ten or fifteen people crowding around her cubicle for a tutorial in things like Blue Mountain Cards, an early e-card site, so they could send an e-card to one of their clients.

That's when Tricia realized that her digital savvy was her opening, and she started exploring how she could get Emmis more involved in the dot-com space. By converting a weakness (youth) into a strength (hipness), Tricia repositioned herself. She leveraged her cultural intelligence to get noticed, and she leveraged her knowledge of the digital trends to get ahead. And let's face it: it helps to also *look* cool while delivering exceptional results.

Men—and the Status Quo—tend to belittle women who are into fashion; many of them treat the whole notion of fashion as frivolous or shallow. We disagree. In fact, we think developing and maintaining a personal style could not be more important.

At the start of Antoinette's career, she was focused on upping her networking game, meeting with anyone and everyone she could who worked in TV. Finally, she was able to set up an informational interview at *The Montel Williams Show*.

It was a good meeting, and Antoinette hoped they would offer her a job on the spot, but there weren't any openings at the time. As Antoinette was walking from the glass-walled conference room toward the exit, the show's executive producer, Diane Rappaport, happened to see Antoinette walking down the hallway and admired how she'd assembled herself. Diane stopped Antoinette to compliment her on the print of her dress, and they started talking. Antoinette knew what she needed to do now: in two sentences, she explained why she wanted to be in TV and why it was her true passion.

Apparently, her style and her confidence made an impression on Diane, because two weeks later, after a PA from *The Montel Williams Show* quit, HR called Antoinette and offered her the job.

That's *cool.*

COMPASSION: HIT THE HEART, STAY IN THE BRAIN

So you've got your confidence and you've got your cool. Now it's time to temper them both with compassion, because you don't want to be cocky or too cool to care.

The Status Quo would have you believe that you always need to be out for yourself, that it's all conflict and strife, that you need to make others feel small for you to feel big. That approach may "work" for *some* people, temporarily at least, but we don't recommend it. More often than not, people who lack compassion fail to live up to their dreams for the simple reason that they don't really understand or know how to read people. That is a serious fucking handicap!

No matter what industry you're in, thinking about what makes other people tick is at the core of everything you do. Compassion leads to connection. If you up your compassion, you'll up your game.

Plus, all Boss Ladies know that you *feel* most alive when you're *feeling* for other people. If cool can stun the Status Quo, then compassion knocks it out cold.

We're both storytellers, even though our medium isn't usually the written word, so take it from us: compassion is the mystery ingredient in all well-backed stories. Stories are *about other people*, and the best ones are generous: they don't just show off the cleverness of the author or the message, they give people a new way to feel, think, or experience the world.

If you want someone to care about you, you need to invite them into your story. And if you want to help someone out, you need to play a supporting role in theirs.

Mom was all about compassion, and she flexed it all the time. We'll talk more about the Matriarchy we grew up in in Part Two, but what you need to know now is that Mom, the Aunts, and Grandma formed a village all their own when we were growing up—almost like a castle with a moat around it—where the motto was all for one and one for all. When someone was having a problem, it was everyone's problem. When someone was celebrating, we were all celebrating.

That's the way we grew up—it was a given that you cared about others and helped them achieve their dreams. We often reaped the benefits of that philosophy when we were little, and it hasn't led us astray as adults. What we learned from watching Mom was that it pays to be genuine—and being genuine is all about being genuinely compassionate.

Sure, you gotta prioritize yourself, make sure you're not spreading yourself too thin, but by practicing compassion, you actually do yourself a great service. All of life is a series of problems, and the more problems you solve—your own and other people's—the better equipped you'll be to succeed in the world.

When Antoinette is designing a product integration as a VP at CBS, she thinks first about how it'll reach viewers in the heart, not the head. Clever might crack a smile, but only compassion will help keep your message alive in people's minds when the day is over. Clever might get you in the door, but only compassion will make people want to invite you to sit and stay awhile.

As OG Maya Angelou says, "People will forget what you said, people will forget what you did, but people will never forget how you made them feel."

Compassion is also rocket fuel for inspiration, just like the first of the Three Cs: confidence. But whereas confidence is about *feeling the power within you*, compassion is about *feeling the power around you*. If you're striving to lift up other people with your work, not only will you think more and think harder about those people and what they care about, but you will also begin to feel that it's more than just your ass on the line. There is great pride in the important work we do for others.

On the Download

Fight like a Swiss Army knife.
A Swiss Army knife has flexibility and mobility, with various tools to confront myriad situations. This is how you need to think about how you approach your work: you are a problem solver.

All success starts from a place of strength.
In everything you do, you need to tap into your core, where your passion and faith reside, so that you can always make your first move with confidence and power.

Find your superpower, then double down on it.
Don't let the Status Quo trick you into thinking you are ordinary. Find your superpower, where your passion and your expertise meet, so that you can start leveraging your unique skills.

Cultivate the 3 Cs

Confidence: Be open to your audacity. If you don't believe in yourself, you can't expect others to believe in you either.

Cool: Hone your cultural intelligence and develop your own unique personal style.

Compassion: Compassion is rocket fuel for inspiration. Clever might crack a smile or get you in the door, but compassion will up your game.

chapter two

Don't Stay in Place, Move into White Space

When we pulled up to Skidmore College in the mid-1990s for freshman orientation in a tiny red Toyota Tercel that sagged under the weight of all our stuff in the trunk, we thought we'd arrived at either (a) a luxury car dealership or (b) a Ralph Lauren photo-shoot. That car was one of many things we were going to share that first year. Another was a cell phone. At the start of college, we didn't have enough money for two phones, so we shared one. You can imagine *that* got complicated—especially with boys—but that's another story.

Since we owned neither a BMW nor a closet full of polo shirts, it took us a little while to find our comfort zone at Skidmore. Kind of like Goldilocks in the story of the Three Bears, we went through a few different groups before we found our tribe. We hung out with the Latinx crew, then the African American crew, and we even tried the ultra-preppy white crew for a day. Pretty soon we realized that we felt most comfortable with a combination of all three—anyone we could learn from, anyone who grew up in a big city, anyone who shared our love of music, and anyone who wanted to *connect*, it didn't matter what color they were.

What did matter, however, was $$$. We didn't have much of it. And to do fun shit in college you need cash.

We'd worked the summer before college, so we had some savings, but that wasn't gonna float us for four years. We got jobs in the library a few times a week to bring in some more cash. But those paychecks didn't stay deposited in our bank accounts very long—we all liked to go out on the weekends to party.

The main nightspot in town was called Peabody's. It wasn't really *our* scene—but it was literally The. Only. Scene. In. Town: flat screens playing sports, singalongs to Guns n' Roses' "Paradise City," sweating beer mugs on the bar. It was fun enough in the beginning, but it got sticky, smelly, and repetitive pretty quick. And no one was out on the dance floor—ever. It felt like we were living in that town in *Footloose*! People were just *standing there*, not dancing, not even bopping their heads, and believe us: there was no hope of hearing any Biggie coming out of that jukebox to get the vibe flowing. If we were gonna blow all our disposable income on pitchers of beer and weak cranberry-vodkas, shouldn't we at least be having a whole lot more fun?

Sure, we could have said, "You know, this isn't our vibe, but there's nothing better, so let's just settle for what exists." That would certainly have been the easiest thing to do. But, as we always say, nothing great is easy. And we were aiming for greatness even then.

So one night walking back from Peabody's we had a conversation.

NETTE
We should host our own party where people
can dance.

> TRISH
>
> That's a good idea.

> NETTE
>
> But where?

> TRISH
>
> What about *there*?

Trish was pointing to a spot called the Golden Grill, an old bar-and-restaurant whose decor was the love child of a 1960s diner and a 1980s strip club.

> NETTE
>
> We'd need to MacGyver that shit.

> TRISH
>
> Obviously.

The Golden Grill was owned by a guy named Todd, a pot-bellied, brown-skinned townie with the friendliest face you'll ever see. Todd would light up like a Christmas tree and wave—"Hi, twins!"—as we walked past on Thursday nights en route to Peabody's. The Golden Grill was always empty, but it was also always blaring dope music.

That night we broke it down for ourselves: the Golden Grill always had good hip-hop and classic soul playing, and a big empty dance floor—but no cool clientele or ambiance. Peabody's was constantly crammed with college kids all clamoring for a beer at the bar while the jukebox played the same cheesy three-chord rock songs. The idea was staring us right in the face. What if we hosted a weekly Thursday night party at the Grill, siphoning off some college kids we knew from Peabody's and making bank in the process?

We pitched the idea to Todd.

> TODD
>
> Skidmore kids? In here? Ain't gonna happen.

> NETTE
>
> If you build it, they will come.

> TRISH
>
> What she said.

And then, since we'd rehearsed it, we went in for the kill.

> TRISH AND NETTE
>
> Give us 50 percent of the cover charge—ten
> bucks a head, and we'll give you the kids.

> TODD
>
> You bring them college kids in here, you got
> a deal.

Our hypothesis was simple: even though everyone seemed relatively fine with Peabody's being the only show in town, once presented with a cooler alternative, they'd go there instead. Were we sure it would succeed? No. But we were sure we were **solving a problem** that needed to be solved—even if our classmates didn't know it yet. And we were confident that we had the skills to pull it off.

For one thing, we knew music, and we knew dancing; remember, Mom had raised us on a steady diet of everyone from Buju Banton and Barbra Streisand to Stevie Nicks and Pat Benatar. We also knew cool: after all, we'd been raised in Brooklyn. We'd been going to clubs like the Tunnel and Palladium since sophomore year in high school. And we knew how to sell: Remember how we'd flipped all those Guess sweatshirts? And, crucially, we also knew what skills we *didn't* have: we weren't DJs.

So we did what you do: we called upon our crew. Early on in the school year, we'd met this spiky-brown-haired dude named Rory from Manhattan, who we knew loved to go to Albany on weekends to hunt for vinyl. We figured that kind of passion was the kind that could be applied to our new venture—and we were right! We got Rory on the phone—speakerphone, of course, seeing as we still had only the one cell—and he jumped at the opportunity to spin for us on Thursdays. He was also ecstatic that there'd finally be an alternative to Peabody's.

We'd had the idea, we'd secured the venue, now we had the music. The only thing that remained was, well, the bodies! How do we get the bodies in the door?

We needed good advertising. So we leaned hard into our superpower, our Twinity, to bill the event as "Doublemint Productions and DJ Ro-Nice Present Thursday Night at the Golden Grill." Clear as day and simple as salt! We spent a few hours on good old Power-Point, then we hit the campus with nothing but a hundred flyers, a staple gun, and two smiles. We gave the bulletin boards at the student center some new wallpaper, then proceeded to talk up our party to anyone who would listen.

The next week, we held our breath and waited. When Thursday night rolled around, we rolled up to the Golden Grill—and found it packed like an MJ concert at Madison Square Garden! Heads were bopping, bass lines were thumping, and DJ Ro-Nice was on the ones-and-twos. Kids were happy, Todd was happy, and we were doubly happy! It was a quadruple win. And we pocketed enough cash to feel well on our way to being able to keep up with the Joneses—or at least to get a second cell phone!

Where there had once been only one option for our friends and classmates looking to socialize and blow off some steam, now there were two. Even though no one had stated a desire for an alternative to Peabody's, we saw a need for something new. So we did what you do: we filled that need ourselves.

To us, it was simple: **if what's needed doesn't exist, create it.**

That's what finding your White Space is all about. We used our skills and passions to create something new, and we changed the social game at Skidmore for our crew and acquaintances in the process. This success gave us lots of confidence to continue to look for our White Space in the years to come.

Finding Your White Space

Now that you know the importance of doubling down on your uniqueness, it's time for you to locate where you can apply it to the greatest effect—that big open space or empty lane where you're gonna accelerate your path forward.

It's time for your superpower to meet opportunity.

It's time for you to seek out what we call White Space.

White Space is an area of opportunity in your professional or creative life where you can double down on your expertise to make a big impact quickly. White Space is like a mountain that's never been scaled. And you have what it takes to get to the top and plant that flag!

Finding your White Space can be about creating a new category or inventing something new, like Phat Farm or Moon Juice. Or it can be about reimagining something that already exists but in a different or better way, like Airbnb or Rent the Runway. White Space is where you can put your unique strengths, skills, and talents to work; it's where you can double down on a problem that no one is solving, a problem that nobody may have even *thought* to solve. White Space is your place to shine. White Space is where you can rethink what you're capable of—and bring to the world something that wasn't there before.

Use classical instruments to play syncopated rhythms and improvised solos—that was jazz. Jazz was White Space!

Attempt to represent one object from all different angles at the same time in a painting—that was Cubism. Cubism was White Space!

Take the one-upmanship of street talk and the Dozens and add in loops from records played on two turntables—that was hip-hop. Hip-hop was White Space!

White Space pushes culture forward.

Keep in mind: there's nothing in the world more valuable than a problem solver. We learned that early on from Mom—securing those tickets to MJ, transforming her old dresses into our Halloween costumes—and we've seen it again and again throughout our careers. Life is full of problems, and if you can find the solution to even just a single one of them, your career will take a giant leap forward. Even coming up with a small improvement to an old way of doing things, or a tweak to an outdated approach, can make all the difference between someone who blends into the background and someone who stands out and gets noticed. And standing out is the name of the game.

Why? Because you have to stand out so you can pull ahead. But to do that you need some room to breathe, operate, and invent. Room to be your best self, your truest self—you know—*your* unique self. Rocking your uniqueness in the White Space: *that's* what's gonna get you eyeballs, accolades, and Escalades.

Right now, there may be something in your way. Yep, you guessed it. The Status Quo. The Status Quo doesn't want you to stand out. The Status Quo wants you to stand back. To stay in line. To wait your turn. The Status Quo wants to keep you as far as possible from your White Space.

"Pay your dues," the Status Quo says. "Follow my lead, put your nose to the grindstone—and then maybe you can get a break!"

Como se dice . . . hell, *no*! The Status Quo may not recognize your brilliance, but that's where you've got the Status Quo beat. The Status Quo can't think outside the box. But you can!

Outside that box is where Boss Ladies like yourself will make your mark. It's where you will draw your X: *I was here*. Outside the box is White Space.

White Space is where the magic happens. White Space is where you'll be recognized for who you are, not held back for who you aren't.

White Space is where you need to be.

Now's the time to let the world in on what you've known for years: you got skills. To do that, you need to find a professional or creative area where you can show off all that you have to offer—and then some. When you apply your unique skills to an overlooked issue, a broken system, or an old problem—or, better yet, when you're first on the scene to anticipate a problem coming around the corner—you will be unstoppable.

It doesn't matter who you are or what you do, White Space is like MasterCard: it's everywhere you want to be.

If you're running your own business as an entrepreneur or freelancing or making art, you need to find your White Space to prove you're **undeniable**.

If you're working within a big company as an intrapreneur, you need to find your White Space to prove you're **indispensable**.

When we entered the workforce, we chose to follow different paths: Antoinette went into TV production, Tricia into marketing and sales. We both worked our asses off when we were starting out, doing what everyone does, what the Status Quo wants us to do: work hard, get things done, and perform flawlessly. We learned the ropes, we took orders, we lived and breathed our job descriptions. We waited our turns, we hoped for promotions, and we toed the line.

The three lies that the Status Quo told us from the beginning were:

- Everyone cares how hard you work.

- Everyone cares about how well you do what's asked of you.

- The people who get to the top are the ones who log the most hours or sweat it out the most.

The three truths we learned really quickly were:

- Most people care more about how *smart* you work.

- Most people care more about how you do what's *not* asked of you.

- The people who get to the top are the ones who stand out, not the ones who sweat it out.

Of course, you need to do everything that's expected of you in your job description. You will need to take meetings you don't want to take, do the paperwork you wish someone else would do, and take on projects that are beneath you.

Everyone does that stuff. That doesn't make you special.

But if all you're doing amazingly well are things that fall into the parameters of the job description that was written for you, you will never become the best at your job—or transcend it. It's that simple. You'll top out. You'll get stuck. Remember, the Status Quo will do everything in its power to keep you in your place. And as long as you continue doing only what is asked of you, as long as you keep trying to blend inconspicuously into the woodwork, as long as you take

No for an answer, you're pretty much letting the Status Quo win. Instead, you need to get out there and unleash your value proposition on the world.

If you're an entrepreneur like Tricia, who has always been drawn to risk and starting her businesses, you need to show that your work is **undeniable**—*you are offering an edge over your competitors* because the service you are providing, or the stand-up routine you are honing, or the product you are selling, is top-of-the-line.

If you're an intrapreneur like Antoinette, you need to show your work is **indispensable**—to perform your role so well by fixing problems, increasing efficiency, or bringing in dollars that *you are offering an edge that no one else can.*

If you're *undeniable* or *indispensable*, then you'll be unstoppable. It's that simple.

And this is simple, too: We believe in you. *You* believe in you. And that's all it takes for you to teach the rest of the world to believe in you, too.

Find Your Edge—Then Use It

Finding your White Space means taking what you're uniquely amazing at—deriving from your superpowers—and applying it to an opportunity out in the world. It starts with asking yourself two simple questions:

QUESTION #1: *What am I good at?*

QUESTION #2: *Where can I apply that skill to make the biggest impact?*

We talked a bit about question #1 in the last chapter: about the importance of locating your superpower and doubling down on it. But here we want to drill down deep as bedrock on *how*. It might sound like a simple question. But often, the simple questions are the hardest ones to answer.

Don't let Bullshit Status Quo notions of *what I should be good at* get confused with the million-dollar question of *what I actually am good at*. And here's the thing: *what you think you should be good at* is almost never the same thing as *what you are good at*. That's because *what you think you should be good at* is in most cases what your parents wanted you to be good at (usually something similar to what *they* were good at—or wished they were) or what the Status Quo wants you to be good at (usually whatever will distract you from doubling down on your true awesomeness and creating change).

Finding your White Space is hard—you will always encounter resistance. We certainly did. While Mom encouraged us to follow our passions and become our best selves, she also not-so-secretly hoped and expected we'd go to graduate school. Like many immigrants who make it in America, Mom believed education—and lots of it—was the One True Path. She—and the rest of our family—sent the message loud and clear: to achieve success you needed a higher degree. Preferably, the highest.

The problem was . . . well, graduate school just wasn't *our thing*.

We didn't want to spend more time in classrooms and labs, we wanted to make the whole world our classroom and our lab!

When we graduated from Skidmore, we told our family we were "deferring" grad school for a year "to get a taste of the working world." Then we threw ourselves into our careers and tried to get as far into them as possible before the rest of the family realized what we were up to. It didn't take our family long to figure out that we *had less-than-zero intention of ever going back to school again*, and we took *heat* for it—molten lava. But over time Mom came around. After all, as we were quick to remind her, Mom, too, had staged her own rebellion against the Status Quo simply by having us when she did. And hadn't she always taught us that it was okay—even *more* than okay—to go against the grain?

She appreciated the point—eventually. She didn't really have a choice, for the simple reason that we proved we could support ourselves and be successful *without* going back to school. Facts don't lie. We showed her that our way worked for us. We showed her that by plunging head first into our careers we had found our White Space: the place where our best selves could shine.

So, where's your White Space? What's your edge, and how can you use those talents to solve a problem or meet a need?

When it comes down to it, your White Space is going to be hanging out somewhere in the intersection of three key factors. The first is your **passion**: what you care about, what drives you. The second is your **achievement**: where you have succeeded already. And the third is your **reputation**: why people come to you, what you are known for.

But remember question #2. Finding your White Space isn't just about knowing what you're good at. It's about figuring where you can *apply that skill to make the biggest impact.* It's about understanding where you are, what others are doing, and how you can push your creative or professional field forward.

First you have to take a critical look at *what everyone else in the space is doing, and how they're doing it.* You need to survey the competitive landscape in order to find your place in it.

This is exactly what Boss Lady Leandra Medine Cohen did when she launched her insanely popular website *Man Repeller.* After graduating college, she planned to go into a career in journalism, like a lot of other very smart and ambitious women. At the same time, she decided to start a fashion blog to keep her writing skills sharp while she worked on getting her feet wet as a reporter. So she did some homework on the competition and asked herself: *What can I do within the existing landscape that no one else is doing?* "I launched around the same time that *Fashion Toast* and *Bryanboy* and *The Sartorialist* and *Street Peeper* were blowing up, and *Man Repeller* was really one of the only fashion blogs that wasn't a street-style blog or a personal style blog that had such a pointed and niche perspective," she once explained. "It was so singularly about one thing: trends that women love and men hate. I really clung to that, and I think that people did, too."

Leandra doubled down on her niche, and it paid off big time. She understood that if you're plotting world domination you need to do your due diligence first. You have to see the world before you can conquer it. And that's how she found her White Space and launched an amazing career. Once you succeed in owning your White Space, you have a great opportunity to plot your next professional move.

White Space exists in all professions, whether you're a publicist, waitress, teacher, manager, coder, or anything else. In every company, there's *always* a better or different way to do things. In every job, there are *always* problems to solve. Everywhere you look, there are *always* new ideas to bring to life. It's up to you, Boss Lady, to find them. Remember: a Boss Lady doesn't follow fashions, she leads them.

Take the example of Anne Wojcicki, CEO and cofounder of 23andMe. This Boss Lady was working on Wall Street as an analyst focusing on the health care industry when she saw a major problem—and a major opportunity—in how the medical community approached the fight against illness and disease.

"The existing health care system is focused on treatment, not on prevention, because prevention doesn't make money," Anne observed. But she knew that prevention could save lots of lives *and* be financially viable if doctors and researchers had a way to access and help people benefit from their genetic makeup. So she quit her Wall

Street job and set out to find a way to address this issue, and ended up creating the most comprehensive database of genetic data ever compiled for human beings.

The Status Quo hadn't seen the need for 23andMe, so Anne did it herself. She saw what the Status Quo couldn't see: that problems = opportunities. And she leveraged her industry knowledge, her venture capital connections, and her sheer, unwavering determination to start a company hell-bent on revolutionizing the world of medicine.

That's White Space!

For many Boss Ladies, White Space is simply where you live and work. Take it from Boss Lady Carly Cushnie, fashion designer and CEO of Cushnie. Carly left her home in London to pursue her childhood dream of working in fashion, first at Parsons School of Design in Paris and then in New York, also interning at Donna Karan, Proenza Schouler, and Oscar de la Renta. Carly and fellow Parsons grad Michelle Ochs founded Cushnie et Ochs in 2008, and the label became renowned for its bold sensuality and sophisticated minimalism, counting Michelle Obama, Beyoncé, Cynthia Nixon, and Gwyneth Paltrow among its fans. As Carly told us, "Michelle and I came together with this idea because we saw there was an aesthetic missing: being minimal but being sexy in a way that's not vulgar." They saw their White Space in the market, and they decided to fill it.

Now that, as of 2018, Carly is on her own, she's working in a new kind of White Space. "Going solo really made me dig deep into what I brought to the table personally and how I could infuse more of that in the existing identity of the brand," Carly told us. While not all of us are successful fashion designers, Carly put her finger on the essence of creating in White Space. We couldn't have put it better ourselves—that's exactly what you need to do, again and again, when trying to make your mark in this world: dig deep, know what you bring to the table, and push your endeavor forward.

But that's not all for Carly. "The fashion industry has the most grueling schedule," she said. "Now with the addition of bridal, I put out six collections a year. How many artists put on six shows in a year or movie directors make six movies in a year? It's definitely not an easy process, but I've always looked at each collection as an evolution, as a building block." Each collection that Carly puts out is a new experiment in White Space, calculating what her customer wants, what looks good to her eye, how much it'll cost the consumer, how it'll look when actually worn, and what else is out there in the market. Carly is a Boss Lady, and we can't wait to see what she designs next.

To find your White Space, ask yourself:

Question #1: **What am I good at?**

(A) What do you care about, what drives you? That's your **passion**.

(B) Where have you succeeded, and how? That's your **achievement**.

(C) Why do people come to you, what are you known for? That's your **reputation**.

Question #2: **Where can I apply that skill to make the biggest impact?**

(A) What is everyone else in the space doing, and how are they doing it?

(B) What makes them successful, and why do people gravitate toward them?

(C) What can you do within the existing landscape that no one else is doing?

Learn the Rules. Then Rewrite Them.

That's exactly what Antoinette did when she took the biggest professional leap of her life.

After years of producing for Montel, Tyra, Rachael Ray, and Nate Berkus, Antoinette decided she needed to make a change at the end of 2011. She knew she wanted more job stability: she was fed up with the uncertainty of TV production, where you're always worrying that a show might get canceled. To figure out what her next move would be, she needed to ID her *edge*—to locate *that one area where she could have the biggest impact.*

She knew she loved reaching people emotionally—inspiring them and connecting with them through storytelling. And she knew what she'd achieved: she had come up with and planned every detail for thousands of segments on everything from school bullying to fashion week; she had worked with a variety of hosts, developing the best content for them and for their audience; and she had always remained up-to-the-minute on trends and culture to keep the shows fresh.

She was confident that she could help convince brands to team up with TV shows to reach their target audience. After all, at *The Tyra Banks Show* she had helped deliver results for top-tier companies that wanted their message expressed seamlessly in the content of the show, and she had also been responsible for producing and securing her own editorial product features. So she placed a bet on herself and decided to try her hand at working for a media company in the branded content wing.

After a brief stint at Martha Stewart Living Omnimedia, where she began to lead branded entertainment and integrations, she doubled down on her decision to commit to branded content and took a job at CBS as the director of branded entertainment in the daytime division.

She had never actually worked on the sales side before, and she was intimidated. During the challenging transition, she repeated one thing to herself over and over again: *I am bringing skills to this role that no one else in this role has ever had.* This was her White Space! She was taking her unique production skills, her understanding of branding, and her love of storytelling into a whole new arena.

Naturally, this was mad work in the beginning! She was constantly flying back and forth between New York, where the office is, and L.A., where they shoot the shows. During her first year, she flew back and forth five times one month. That's a lot of frequent flyer miles, pairs of cheap earphones, and cardboard dinners! Antoinette was doing it all—cold-calling new clients to pitch integration opportunities, building a business within a business, putting process and procedures in place, generating creative ideas, and executing the proposals; she was working till eight or ten most nights, trying to get it all done. Ironically, one of the reasons she left TV was that she didn't want to work around the clock, but this was different. Why? Because she knew that she'd found her White Space—and she knew that **once you're in White Space, you need to own it.**

Soon she got a chance to put all her hard work to the test. A Fortune 500 company was interested in possibly doing an integration with *The Talk* to promote one of the most successful beauty brands on the market today, which meant that Antoinette needed to come up with some compelling reasons why *The Talk* could help the company reach their target demographic.

She was in the hot seat twice over: she needed to prove her worth to CBS *and* she needed to prove to the company that CBS daytime could deliver results.

This was a big *challenge*: come up with a creative idea for a huge global company. But by the same token it was a big *opportunity*: come up with a creative idea for a huge multinational company.

This was where she needed to shine. So she did what you do: she surveyed the landscape. She studied what the company had done in the past, how they had successfully reached their customers, and she cross-referenced this with what she knew *The Talk* already did extremely well. Then she looked for ways that she could bring new ideas to the table from her old jobs. She was going to Swiss Army knife this!

Antoinette came up with five integration ideas and showed her work to her boss, Jared.

"This is really good," he told her, "but usually when we send a response, our proposals just have one solid idea. Just the main course."

Antoinette said: "Oh, I come from a different school of thought. Where I come from you need to offer a buffet. I figure: You never know who's going to be in the room, so you don't know what's going to resonate. I want to offer the basic 'How To' segment, where we get some real people with fine lines and wrinkles to demonstrate the product, but I also want to open their minds to see that their message can get out there in other ways. Here's one idea: What if we did a game show infused with pop culture?"

"That's a great idea!" he replied. And then came the "but." "But I just think this company tends to be more conservative, so they're probably going to go with the 'How To' segment. I'm sorry. You put so much work into this."

Jared assumed that was the end of the story. But clearly he didn't know who he was dealing with! Antoinette proceeded to inform him that she respectfully disagreed and that she was going to go ahead and do her proposals her way, as she had planned.

Learn the rules. Then rewrite them.

When the proposal went out, the company loved the ideas, and *The Talk* won the integration deal over several other non-CBS daytime shows. By offering a menu of ideas—instead of just one main course option—she demonstrated her competitive edge: *If you do business with me, you will get high-quality options.*

Soon enough, Antoinette was bringing in so many big brands—and so many stacks of bills—that CBS had no idea what they'd ever done without her. That's when Antoinette knew she had worked her White Space game like a G: she'd made herself **indispensable**.

Now, as VP of branded entertainment, Antoinette is in the unique role of taking two fixed stories from two different authors—a particular brand's identity, the particular show's identity—and merging them into one seamless integration that works for the brand, the TV show, and the intended audience. With expectations and stakes as high as they are, Antoinette finds inspiration in aiming for the heart, where passions reside.

Learn the rules. Then rewrite them.

This is exactly what Tricia did when she took the biggest professional leap of *her* life—coming up with the idea for Narrative_.

In 2009 Tricia joined Russell Simmons's media company Global Grind. It wasn't long before she became copresident, relaunched the platform, led over a hundred campaigns for brands like Pepsi, Toyota, and AT&T, and grew revenue by 500 percent. Because of all the success that Global Grind had enjoyed with her at the helm, Fast Company called her Russell's "secret weapon." So when the massive media company Interactive One arrived at a joint venture deal with Russell and his partner Osman Eralp to house the content team of Global Grind in their New York office, Tricia had to plot her next move.

Tricia didn't want to do more of the same, and *especially* not more of the same working underneath a big corporate umbrella. She wanted to hit upon the Next Big Thing. With a new corporate overlord, she knew it'd be harder to innovate, experiment, and take chances the way she had been able to do at Global Grind. Maybe it was time to go out and look for her next White Space.

One rainy day she stood in Russell's forty-third-floor office: wood panels, wooden desk, wooden bookcase. She peered down at the wet city beneath her and reflected on the situation.

> TRICIA
>
> Isn't this some shit?

> RUSSELL
>
> Whatya mean?

> TRICIA
>
> I worked my ass off to increase revenue, find new clients, and help you reimagine the business so successfully that you and Osman are about to make a big deal and a boatload of money and I'll be out of a job!

> RUSSELL
>
> Ha. Yeah, when you put it like that. Okay, well, what do you wanna do?

> TRICIA
>
> Hmm, what do I wanna do? Give me forty-eight hours and I'll tell you.

Forty-eight hours later Tricia marched back into his office and announced that she wanted to launch a new type of ad agency—one that was unlike any others out there.

Russell looked up, saw in her eyes that she was as serious as a heart attack, and said, "Wow, okay. Let's be partners. Something like 70/30 or 60/40. Let's keep talking once we close the deal and get Global Grind installed over at Interactive One."

70/30, 60/40? Tricia thought. *That's not "partners" where I come from. And "keep talking"? I want to make this happen, like, now.*

So, while still running Global Grind by day, Tricia began spending her nights and weekends refining her idea for a new kind of agency. Naturally, she started by surveying the competitive landscape. This was her thinking:

- Creative agencies are telling great stories, but they lack tech . . .

- Innovation agencies are coming up with great products and ideas, but they don't know how to bring them to life . . .

- Influencer agencies know how to identify talent, but they don't wrap them in a unique story . . .

- Tech agencies design and develop amazing products, but they lack a connection to the human experience . . .

- Content and production agencies can execute ideas, but they don't provide an end-to-end, real-time, agile, and flexible solution for all content types . . .

Tricia saw her White Space: a new kind of agency that broke down these silos, combining storytelling with technology. Not only would it help brands tell stories in novel ways and connect with new and existing customers, but it would also leverage technology to find new ways of *delivering* those stories. Part agency, part innovation lab, it wouldn't just be about *telling* a story: it would also be about allowing people to *experience* the story. She wanted to deliver groundbreaking campaigns and monetizable IP. She wanted to flip the agency model on its head and spin it all around, like a B-girl, but without messing up her hair. Tricia had worked with agencies and brands, and she knew that somewhere between the antiquated rules of advertising and the enduring appeal of entertainment, between the transience of cultural movements and the unknown possibilities of technology, there was a White Space unexplored where amazing, boundary-pushing work could be made. This new agency would define, rewrite, and perfect a brand's entire narrative. That was it!

The name of this new agency, she decided, would be Narrative_.

Tricia called upon her crew and got hooked up with all kinds of contacts: she met with an angel venture capital investor in New York, and she set up a meeting with a multimillionaire friend who was also part of an investor group. This investor liked it a lot and said he could raise the $1.5 million Tricia needed to get Narrative_ off the ground.

This—people willing to give her money!—was all the validation that she needed. Now she was ready to start negotiating.

Back in Russell's office a few days later, she stood again by the windowsill, where all the framed pictures of Russell and celebrities/politicians stood. Tricia turned to Russell and Osman, drawing a deep breath.

> **TRICIA**
> Remember the agency idea we were
> talking about where we'd not only redefine
> storytelling but also the means by which
> stories are told, creating passive revenue
> streams through monetizable IP?

> **OSMAN**
> I like monetizable IP.

> **RUSSELL**
> Yeah, I remember. It's a great idea!
> I love it! We'll be partners.

> TRICIA
>
> Right, so, well, that's the thing.
> I've secured funding to launch it.

> RUSSELL
>
> Whoa, wait, from who?

Tricia told him.

> RUSSELL
>
> Are you serious?

> TRICIA
>
> Does it look like I'm playing?

Russell and Osman said they would talk it over and made Tricia promise not to take any money until they got back to her.

That was a Thursday. On Saturday, when Tricia was out to brunch with Antoinette and some other Boss Ladies, she glanced down at her phone. Three missed calls. From Russell. She phoned him back on the spot.

Russell was calling to tell her that he'd been thinking. "Forget all about the investor," he said. "We'll be full partners and I'll give you the $1.5 million out of my own pocket. Let's do this!"

And that's how Narrative_ came to be! Tricia was starting her own company! In just a few weeks she had managed to take a small seed of an idea and turn it into a reality. She was moving full steam into her glorious White Space.

(Tricia had made herself *undeniable*.)

Tricia has made herself *undeniable* as CEO of her creative and tech agency, Narrative_ (which Hollywood hit-maker and producer Will

Packer acquired in 2017). As she always tells new clients, "We go for hearts, not eyeballs. We connect with the user on an emotional plane, then hit them with the cool factor." It's her one-two punch.

We both took big chances with our careers striking out in new directions: Antoinette into branded content and Tricia into a new business. While these were big leaps into the unknown, we'd both evaluated our strengths, done our market research, and doubled down when we saw our opening. That's how White Space works.

We didn't want to wait for our turns, or for our numbers to be called, or for someone to give us permission. We just *did*—by following our rules, our way. And you can too. That's the way into the White Space.

Bet against the Status Quo.

Don't confuse output with outcome.

Don't confuse motion with action.

Don't confuse activity with achievement.

Be the author of your destiny.

On the Download

White Space will set you free.
White Space is an area in your creative or professional life where you can apply your unique skills and passion to solving an old problem or meeting a new need.

If what's needed doesn't exist, create it.
This is the basic principle of White Space. White Space is all about seeing the problems and opportunities that no one else sees.

White Space pushes culture forward.
On a grand scale, White Space is where new inventions happen and new modes of expression are created. Think about White Space on the biggest level and apply that to whatever you're trying to achieve.

First, learn the rules. Second, rewrite them.
You gotta learn your chromatic scales before you play free-form jazz, and you need to learn the basics before you get to the Next Level. Pay attention to how the game is played, and then you can go about changing it.

Once you're in White Space, you need to own it!
Once you ID your White Space, you need to hustle hard and double down on that one opportunity where you have a calculable advantage.

Make yourself undeniable/indispensable.
Whether you're an entrepreneur or you work for an established company, you need to prove your worth and your point of differentiation. Your results will make everyone take notice—which will make you unstoppable.

chapter three

Don't Just Compete, Play the Long Game

When Antoinette started out as a production assistant, she was making $25,000 a year. That kind of money didn't get you very far in New York City in the late 1990s, but Antoinette found a way to make it work, even if it meant eating through her meager savings, because her Long Game was to produce. Antoinette knew that to make the biggest dreams come true you need to work your all-out hustle.

When you're just starting out in TV, or most fields for that matter, it's a baptism by fire—and it's not for the faint of heart. You're responsible for researching, booking, and interviewing guests, celebs, and experts, pitching story ideas, culling news footage, supervising crews and shoots in the field, raising the production value while keeping the production costs low, and, oh yes, writing scripts. And this was before the days of the full-blown Internet—or even halfway decent computers. In fact, Antoinette had only a word processor—basically a glorified electronic typewriter. And it used floppy disks! Which meant that she couldn't simply type a few search terms into Google to find ideas or research stories; she actually had to flip through physical copies of newspapers and magazines, one by one.

Point is, the gig was hard work: Antoinette sometimes didn't even have the time to go home at night, opting instead for the one-star luxury sleep pod she made for herself under her desk, atop the itchy corporate carpet. At least on those days, she didn't need to set an alarm: the morning chorus of vacuum cleaners was more than enough to get her off the floor.

This was a tough time. She wasn't making very much money and she was still at the bottom of the ladder. And sometimes she felt like she was getting stepped on! But she knew she couldn't focus on all those people stomping all over her, trying to keep her in her place. What sustained her through the dark times was her knowledge that (1) she deserved to rise up to become a full-fledged producer and (2) she *would* rise up to become a full-fledged producer. Everything else was irrelevant.

Over time, Montel Williams noticed Antoinette's passion and her work ethic. He saw how she got things done, how she stayed late to attend to the minor details of the next day's show—coordinating everything from what the guests were going to wear to how graphics would be displayed. It can be tempting to assume that minutiae doesn't matter when you're working toward your end goal. But in fact, when you're playing the Long Game, the small details matter even more. They're what help you keep your head up and keep you from veering off course.

Antoinette didn't always love spending hours and hours pre-interviewing a pool of guests to determine who would be the most compelling, or spending hours and hours fact-checking their stories. And she most definitely preferred her fluffy bed with pillows and any-number-of-thread-count sheets to the zero-thread-count, dusty office carpet with Brillo-pad softness. But she tried not to get too caught up in all that. She tried not to say to herself: *Why am I working so hard and not going anywhere? This is beneath me.* What she tried to say to herself was: *I am working hard to get where I want to go. It is not beneath me, but soon it will be behind me.*

And eventually it was. In 2006, Antoinette moved over to a new position, producing for Dr. Keith Ablow. She had moved up the ranks in her five and a half years at *The Montel Williams Show* and was ready to diversify her skill set and challenge herself by producing for a different type of show. Then, in early January 2017, just after returning from a rare vacation—a Christmas trip to the Bahamas with Tricia— she got the news: *The Dr. Keith Ablow Show* was getting canceled. And she was out of a job.

That night, back at the two-bedroom apartment that we shared on Sixteenth between Fifth and Sixth, Antoinette was splayed across Tricia's bed—whenever one of us was down, we'd be in the other's room talking it out—in Full Distress Mode. Her show getting canceled had not been part of her master plan. She had worked so hard to get as far as she had, and now it felt like she was all the way back to square one.

NETTE

What am I going to do now? I can't keep doing this.

TRISH

Don't forget your Long Game. You gotta go after that Emmy! You're gonna find another job. And you're gonna find another job after that. You're going to climb your way to the top, one job at a time. Remember: where you are today isn't where you'll be tomorrow.

And she was right. It's not like that new job just magically came knocking at the door at that moment (that was the delivery guy with the Thai food—pad thai!), but Tricia's words were a much-needed reminder that life is all about the Long Game. And when you double down on that mentality, it's easier to get right back in the game after being knocked down. And that's exactly what Antoinette did. She got back in there and played her heart out.

See, the people who truly kick ass here on Planet Earth—who achieve success on their terms and are able to enjoy what that success brings—are the ones who get that life is all about the Long Game. They're playing it, and they're playing to win. This chapter is all about how to double down on your Long Game.

After all, life's a journey—you're a tiny baby, you're a fierce little girl, you're a rebellious teenager; you're soul-searching, you're finding your passions, you're learning, you're falling in love; you lose; you cry, you win; and then your legacy lives on. That's how it all goes.

To get anywhere in life, you need to figure out two things ASAP: (1) where you wanna go, and (2) how you're gonna get there. Worry about the other stuff later. Sure, you'll have to pack your bags, pick out an outfit (or five), book all your flights, and find an Airbnb, but none of that stuff matters unless you commit to those two things. It sounds simple, but it's not. So many young women have only vague notions of where they really want to end up and even vaguer notions of how they're planning on getting there. And so many start out knowing more or less where they want to go and how to get there, but lose their sense of direction somewhere along the way. Why is that?

Because the Status Quo *wants* you to lose your way, so it constantly barrages you with two contradictory stories about success and how to get it. Both of these are designed to knock you off balance and distract you from thinking about the Long Game.

First, the Status Quo Myth Machine imbues the people at the

top—our modern business heroes like Jeff Bezos or Sheryl Sandberg or Elon Musk—with a superhuman, even godlike quality, as if to say, *This'll never be you*. The Status Quo holds these people up on a diamond-studded pedestal, talks about them like they were *born* to be successful—like they're invincible, untouchable—and, what's more, good luck trying to duplicate their model. That kind of success doesn't befall mere mortals like you.

These people seem to possess magic you don't. And it's not just the multibillionaires. This dynamic happens on a smaller scale, too: we're guessing that within your industry and probably your company there are people at the top who are doing what you want to do, while making it seem like they were destined to do it, effortlessly. Like it's no big deal. You can't remember a time when they weren't calling the shots. In which case it must've always been so.

Listen: that's the Status Quo talking.

At the same time, the Status Quo loves to tell you stories about another kind of successful person: those people from humble beginnings who made it big—and changed the world overnight with their *huge* idea! They just woke up one fine morning, they had an idea in the shower, and the next day they were being listed on the New York Stock Exchange! IPO party—champagne and chocolate and cigars for everyone! These people are talked about in a breathless and mythic way, too, as if to say, *This'll never be you*.

These people—and here we're talking the Silicon Valley Bros—seem to possess magic you don't. They are the new masters of the universe—and they're only twenty-four! They have it all, and now there's none left for you.

Listen: that's the Status Quo talking.

The Status Quo loves shining a light on these two mythical stories—the Born Leader, the Overnight Success—because it lumps the majority of us in the middle. And the middle, well, that's where people get stuck. It's where they buy into the Bullshit Status Quo idea that they'll never get where they're going anyway, so why bother?

F that! The middle? We don't see any middles here. We see a journey headed toward a destination. We see one step after the other after the other. The middle? The only thing we're in the middle of is taking over the world!

So let's start thinking about the Long Game mentality—what *your* destination is, and how you're going to hustle your way there by standing out, speaking up, and delivering the goods—again and again.

We know it's scary to say to yourself, let alone the rest of the world, "I want to be X." To declare your true intention can feel like the old high school nightmare of showing up for a class presentation bare-ass naked. That's because the Status Quo unnerves us—it gets inside our heads. You know, that snippy little voice that says stuff like "You can't *honestly* think you'll someday be CEO, do you?" That's the Status Quo talking.

So many of us have a voice like that inside us, prompting us to question if we deserve to be where we are or where we're intending to go. It's what they call Imposter Syndrome, and it happens because as perceptive, ambitious women we are sometimes so focused on all the skills and accomplishments we see in those around us—most often men with power—that we forget all about all the successes *we* have had and all the superpowers that *we* possess. And so we undercut ourselves by saying, *I won't apply for that job; I'm not qualified.* Or *I won't volunteer to give that presentation; I'm not prepared.* Or *I won't ask that question; I'll sound stupid.* We box ourselves into a limited domain that feels safe and comfortable but doesn't leave us any room to grow or to take that step. And when we do enjoy some success, we can downplay it as a fluke—once again undercutting ourselves and not believing that our achievements are proof enough of our skills.

But Imposter Syndrome isn't the only pitfall that can derail our Long Game. Just as the Born Leader Myth gives rise to **Imposter Syndrome**, the Overnight Success Myth can trigger what we call **Superiority Syndrome.** That's where you look around and see only your colleagues' and bosses' shortcomings, conclude that you are far more talented and qualified in every way, and thus assume you should shoot straight to the top right now. So instead of acting unsure of yourself, you act oversure of yourself—at the expense of no one but yourself.

Don't get us wrong: we *want* you to assert your confidence and double down on your skills to move forward and get ahead. But there's a world of difference between confidence and arrogance, and getting ahead doesn't mean *skipping* ahead without having taken the time to really learn and hone the necessary skills. (Remember: first, learn the rules; second, rewrite them.) We want you to score big by playing your best hand when it really counts, and sometimes that means biding your time. When you see the headlines about the latest billion-dollar IPO, or the next hot start-up "moving fast and breaking things," or the latest disruption to a once-stable industry, it can be easy to assume that all it takes to succeed is one idea and a loud voice. It's true that both those things are necessary to be heard, but you also need to listen and learn, watch and wait—so that you can make your best move at the right time.

In other words, it's all about having the Long Game mentality. Because when you keep your head up and focus on the destination over the horizon, you'll be more patient with yourself and with the steps it takes to get there.

The Long Game is what it's all about.

But you gotta be in it to win it.

To Live Up to Your Dreams, Put Them Down in Writing

We both graduated from college with our heads full of big ideas—and even bigger dreams. For us, there was a lot riding on finding our lanes and punching the gas. Remember: we'd told that white lie to Mom and the rest of the Fam about "taking a year off before going to graduate school." We had to prove to them, to each other, and to ourselves that we could make things happen when the rubber met the road.

If we were going to get anywhere, we knew we needed to pick a distant goal to reach. We call this our North Star. It's what you always keep your eyes on so that you always keep moving forward, in the direction of the freedom you crave and the cash-dollars you deserve. If you take your eyes off the North Star and look down at the road in front of you, you'll end up stalled on the side of the road, worrying about how long it is and how far you have to go.

After graduation, we each set our sights on different stars, but the effect was the same: we stayed focused on getting to our destinations, trying not to get distracted by the little bumps along the way. And through it all, we always tried to keep in mind one thing: **where you are today isn't where you'll be tomorrow.**

Antoinette's dream was to become a TV producer for the best shows on daytime television and to win an Emmy for her work before the age of thirty-five. She wanted to tell big, moving stories to millions of female viewers, reaching and connecting with them emotionally and intellectually. And she wanted to help increase the number of female guests on those shows, so more women watching at home could see themselves represented on screen. As we always say, *You can't be what you can't see.*

So the first thing Antoinette did after graduation was get out a piece of paper and write down the words: *I want to become a TV producer and win an Emmy before I'm thirty-five.* No matter how much you might resist, you must put your dream down on paper. Writing it down is the first step in committing to it.

But as with any journey, once you choose a destination, you have to map out a plan for reaching it. So from there, she worked backward. *What steps will I have to take to get there?*

Well, she thought, if you want to produce, you first need to associate-produce for a few years. If you want to associate-produce for a few years, you first need to be a production assistant for a few years. If you want to be a production assistant for a few years, you need to get your foot in the door at a production company. That can be the biggest challenge: breaking down that first barrier to entry.

Okay, Nette said to herself, *that's where I'll start.* And so she did.

Tricia's dream was to become the CEO of her own company and have a million dollars in the bank by the age of forty. She wanted to be a Boss Lady of her own design, with a team of smart, ambitious people working to make an impact—and have a corner office with a view of Central Park or the Statue of Liberty. So she worked backward from Name on the Door. *What steps will I have to take to get there?*

Tricia found her passion in sales—she loved both the art of the sell and the art of connection—and she figured that if you want to get your name on the door and be a CEO of an ad agency, you need to be a president for a while. If you want to be president for a while, you need to be VP of digital sales and marketing. If you want to be VP of digital sales and marketing, you need to be a director of integrated sales. If you want to be a director of integrated sales, you need to be a sales rep. If you want to be a sales rep, you need to get your foot in the door at a media company. That can be the biggest challenge: breaking down that first barrier to entry.

Okay, Tricia said to herself, *that's where I'll start.* And so she did.

We're both big-time believers in putting dreams down on paper. When you do, (1) you start to visualize their eventual reality and (2) you become accountable. It may seem basic, but there are plenty of studies showing that when you write things down you make them easier to accomplish. After all, those are your dreams that you put into writing—and now they're staring you back in the face saying, "Make me come true!" And you will.

We're also big believers in holding ourselves—and each other—accountable. We were lucky to have each other in the early years to buoy each other's spirits and help each other keep our eye on our North Star. Committing to *our* version of success and fulfillment freed us from the expectations of the Status Quo. These were *our* dreams, not anyone else's. That's how you double down on your dream: saying it aloud, telling a friend, and writing it down.

But if you want to win at the Long Game, it's not enough just to set your sights on the North Star. You also have to map out specific goals you want to achieve along the way. That's the second step. Your goals are the difference between achievement and activity. Activity just means you're doing *something,* but achievement means you're doing *your thing.* Remember, just because you're busy doesn't mean you're effective. Effective is when everything you do is in line with the goals you've set for yourself.

Just as we're big believers in putting our Big Dreams down on paper, we're also fans of mapping our goals out on paper—everything from our five-year growth plans to our to-do lists for the day. To-do lists are the Long Game of your daily life. They are your daily maps. They help you see how far you need to travel to get to where you want to be by the end of the day. And to-do lists help you keep your short-term goals aligned with your longer-term dreams by breaking down what has to be done into individual days and weeks. Some people knock to-do lists—usually the same people who can't seem to accomplish the things written on theirs—but we find there's no better tool for getting that shit done. It's old school—and it works.

Our love of lists is shared by Boss Lady Lacy Phillips, founder and CEO of To Be Magnetic. Through her website and workshops, Lacy teaches people how to harness their focus and manifest what they want in life—and she's all about lists. As Lacy told us, "Lists to me are everything. Lists make us get really clear about what we want. They're our blueprints and our road maps. If your desires are wishy-washy, then wishy-washy things will come to you. If you're specific about what you want, you will learn to get it." When Lacy is working with clients trying to manifest the life they want, unblocking themselves from years of outmoded thinking and expanding their own self-worth, she's always telling them to put it in writing.

Antoinette learned early on as a TV producer that you need to be organized AF to keep all your tasks and research straight. In fact, no matter what kind of job you do, you need to be on top of your shit—or else your shit's on top of you. **You can't rely on wishful thinking, you have to rely on listful thinking.** As we always like to say, there are two types of people in this world: those who make lists and those who don't. You're either crossing something off a list or *getting* crossed off a list. The world is a tough and crazy place, so you gotta impose order on it in every way you can—big and small, short and long term.

Ask yourself: What are you doing today that's going to get you where you want to be at the end of the week? What are you doing this month that's going to get you closer to your North Star this year?

Asking ourselves these questions not only keeps us focused on the Long Game but also serves as a daily reminder that we are strong and powerful, that we're going places. Which we are—to the top! And so are you.

Keep Your Head Up

When life gets crazy, it can be easy to take your eyes off the prize. There's all the work you have to do for you. There's all the work you have to do for your boss. There's family drama, there's relationship drama, there's coworker drama. And then there's that chorus of self-doubt running through your head that you can't seem to turn off.

All of these things are textbook definitions of the Short Game. But here's the thing about the Short Game. The Short Game is where the Status Quo is king—it's where the Status Quo wins every time. In Vegas, the House wins when you get distracted by flashing lights and free cocktails; in life, the Status Quo wins when you get distracted by all the people and drama around you.

We get it. It's human nature to pay attention to everyone around us. It's human nature to want to be *liked* by everyone around us. And it's human nature to compare ourselves to everyone around us, to be jealous of the people who become successful more quickly, or to give in to the fears that other people project onto us. But the more we're hung up on what everyone else is doing, the less we're able to focus on what matters: *us*.

We think about the Long Game as being like a long-distance race. Sometimes you might be tempted to look in front of you, where you'll see people moving forward and further ahead. Other times, you'll have the urge to glance to either side of you where you see people catching up to you and gaining speed. Or you might think it's a good idea to look over your shoulder; you see people behind lapping at your heels. It feels like you're not moving at all.

Well, hold the phone! We don't run track, but we know one of the most fundamental rules: never look at the other runners, not the ones behind you or alongside you or even in front of you! If you look back, you're toast. You just lost a ton of time in a race where there's none to lose. If you're focusing on the other runners, you won't be concentrating fully on you. And that's what you need to do to win. It's that simple. **The Long Game is about you, not anyone else.**

Take it from Tori Bowie. Tori knows what winning is about; she's currently one of the fastest female sprinters on Planet Earth. But she wasn't always this fast—or this focused.

Tori was born in 1990 in Sand Hill, Mississippi, a town with zero traffic lights, a good twenty miles from the nearest highway. In high school, she decided to make something of herself and see the world. So she doubled down on her passion for sports, joining the basketball and track teams. Turned out, she was a pretty damn good sprinter, winning two state championships in the 100m and 200m dashes and going on to earn an athletic scholarship to the University of Southern Mississippi. The girl could run like the wind.

She'd found her White Space.

Then, in 2012, she saw a broadcast of the Olympics for the first time. She was blown away—not just by the incredible athletes but by the energy, the harmony, the spectacle of it all. She pointed at the TV and said to herself: *I want to go there.*

She'd found her North Star.

Tori trained and raced and trained some more; she won some big races and lost some big ones, too. She pushed herself to her limits, and then she pushed harder still. Sure, there were disappointing times—times when she was defeated in body and spirit, her muscles exhausted, her soul drained. But she never quit. Tori never took her eyes off the horizon. She didn't slow down to look at other runners, not even for a second. She focused on her game and on getting to her destination: the Olympics. As Tori says, "The journey will not be easy, not even close to easy. Just trust it. Trust the process. Whatever comes along, try to conquer it. And move on to the next thing. What I try to practice is: stay in my own lane. I just try to stay focused on Tori."

In 2016, her philosophy paid off.

Only four years after seeing the Olympics for the first time on a little TV in her Sand Hill living room, she was now *on the TV*, in the Olympic stadium in Rio de Janeiro, competing on the world stage, with all her proud friends and family back in Sand Hill watching her running for her country on that same tiny TV.

And did she let them down? Hell no!

Tori took a bronze medal in the 200m, a silver medal in the 100m, and a gold medal in the 4x100m relay. Yes, you read that right: gold, silver, and bronze. That's literally all the medals there are! And she did it by *staying in her own lane* and *keeping a laser focus on the finish line.* That's what you have to do to achieve your dreams. Because the second you take your eyes off the prize and your head out of the Long Game, that's when you'll start to lose your edge, your speed, your momentum. The second your head gets caught up in the Short Game, that's when the Status Quo pulls ahead.

Aim High, Go Far

Ursula Burns is a true Boss Lady. She'd spent her entire career at Xerox, starting with a summer internship and working all the way up to CEO. (You know you're a Boss Lady when the company you run has become a verb.) Growing up in public housing on the Lower East Side, Ursula didn't have a whole lot of role models. What she did have was doubters, and plenty of them. As she once recalled in an essay for the Lean In organization, "Many people told me I had three strikes against me: I was black. I was a girl. And I was poor."

Now, some people in her situation might have responded by setting their sights low, taking comments like these as proof of the Status Quo myth that "success just isn't for me." But not Ursula. She responded by setting her sights high. Like, corner office high.

Early in her career at Xerox, an executive named Wayland Hicks called Ursula into his office. *I'm about to get reprimanded or fired*, she thought to herself. A few weeks prior, she'd walked right up to him after a meeting about diversity initiatives and called him out for giving credence to the suggestion that diversity implied a lowering of standards. Rather than wonder what this very junior-level person— that is, junior-level African American woman—was doing challenging him, a seasoned (white) executive, Hicks was impressed. He saw that she had fire, and he had heard that she was a hard worker with a commitment to quality—which is why he called her in that day to ask her to become his new executive assistant.

At first, Ursula didn't see his offer as an opportunity. She wanted to be working her way up the ladder, not answering phones and scheduling meetings. But then she realized that this was actually an incredible chance to learn about how the company was run; after all, if she wanted to someday *be* at the top, she needed to know how it looked from the top. This was her chance to find out. Sure, she wouldn't be operating the levers of power, but she would get to study the way others did. Her motto was: If you want your name on the door, you have to know the business inside and out. So she made a commitment to listen, learn, and absorb all she could. Plus, she figured, when she was ready to move up she could work her new executive-level connections, rather than duking it out among the other entry-level employees.

She made a bet that over time this strategy would pay off. And it did. In 2009 she became the CEO of Xerox—and also the first female African American CEO of a Fortune 500 company!

Ursula understood that you gotta **know your future prize—and double down on getting it.** That's the Long Game.

Similarly, back when Antoinette was starting out at CBS, she was working crazy hard hours: in part because she wanted to stand out and impress, in part because she wanted to learn all she could about the company, and in part because she had set her sights high and knew that it really takes effort to rise to the top, especially in fields like media and television. Pretty soon her boss noticed her long hours and was concerned; he didn't want her to burn out in her first year on the job! Antoinette took his words to heart. And from that point on, she did what you do: she started asking for help. Pretty soon, CBS hired someone to train to help her execute on her ideas. And not long after that, Antoinette started to get her personal life back. But she had zero regrets. She was playing the Long Game, and when you do that you sometimes have to sacrifice the short term to get what you want.

The higher you aim, the higher you'll rise. Why? The bigger the goal, the harder you'll work to get there. And the more you believe you have what it takes, the more likely you'll be to succeed. Generally, if you imagine yourself at the top, it'll be easier for other people to imagine you there, too. When you're reaching for the stars, you need to know you deserve your dream.

The Shortest Distance Isn't Always a Straight Line

When you're playing the Long Game, sometimes you have to take detours to acquire skills or experiences. But it's worth it, because it means that when you do really arrive—and you will!—you'll know how to handle your shit.

Tricia learned this lesson firsthand after she'd been at Emmis Communications for two years. She'd cut her teeth signing accounts, pitching her creative services, and bringing in a ton of new business, but she wasn't rising up or breaking out of the old and into the new. Even though she was consistently proving her ability to deliver the dollars, the bosses were not responding in kind. So she went out in search of greener pastures.

In the end, she came back with four viable offers: from CBS Radio and Clear Channel (this was before they merged) to work in the same space she was in, only for a bigger paycheck, and from AOL and Excite (the number three Internet portal at the time), where she could learn a new skill set and gain a different kind of experience.

While the bigger and more established old-school media players were offering more money, Excite was offering the opportunity to really grow. This was in 2000, during the first dot-com boom when the World Wide Web was the Wild Wild West, so Tricia knew it was a chance to learn on the fly and to learn *to* fly. The short-term move would have been to take the money from Clear Channel and continue to climb the familiar ladder. But Tricia kept her eyes on the long-term goal and took less money to go to Excite, where she believed she'd grow in ways that would make her a better hire in the short term, a better leader in the medium term, *and* better equipped to one day achieve her long-term goal of running her own company.

At Excite, Tricia became fully immersed in the digital space, implementing integrated advertising programs across multiple platforms (narrowband, broadband, wireless, and offline), educating clients on the potential for digital campaigns, creating measurement frameworks, and negotiating national and local advertising contracts for targeted markets. Things were happening so quickly! And then, after less than a year at Excite, once she'd gotten a good handle on digital ad products and delivering ROI, guess who came calling with guarantees of more money and more power? Emmis. That's right. They wanted her back.

While walking away had clearly been the right decision, Tricia now saw White Space back at Emmis: she could take what she'd learned at the new media company and inject it into the old media company. Plus, they were offering her control of a brand-new division: the digital division. *Heading up a new department*, she thought to herself. *That would be a perfect approximation of running my own business.* So she went—first developing a new business model, then leading the division to create cross-platform campaigns for PUMA, EA Sports, iTunes, and Fox. It turned out to be a smart move—and one that brought her one giant leap closer to that corner office.

But after a few more years at Emmis, she was feeling that itch again. So when Russell Simmons came along and offered Tricia the chance to help run his fledgling media company Global Grind, Tricia was intrigued. Around that time she also got an offer at another well-established company that came with a hefty raise, which meant that she had a pretty tough decision to make. So she checked in with her North Star again: run a business and have a million in the bank by forty. Was that gonna happen working longer at Emmis—or at any traditional company? No way. People thought she was crazy for turning down the cash and the pedigree, but at Global Grind she would be getting access and exposure to a mogul, equity in the company, and the freedom to experiment. That was her ticket. So she went.

And then after four years at Global Grind, Tricia pitched Russell on the idea for Narrative_. At that point, finally, she became the CEO of her own company.

Success Is Sweeter When You Recall Where You've Been

On Day One of Narrative_, Tricia came into work, rode the elevator to the ninth-floor office she had picked out for herself, sat down, and made a list (we told you, we love lists!). She wrote down her five-year goals for the new company she'd started, and for herself. This way, she figured, even when the going got tough and she was working long-ass hours, she could remind herself *why* she was working so hard: to accomplish everything on that list.

Four and a half years later, after she had just closed a deal for Narrative_ to be acquired by Hollywood producer Will Packer's media company, she looked back at the same list again.

Create IP. **(CHECK)**

Be recognized for disrupting the advertising industry. **(CHECK)**

Put a new consumer brand on the map. **(CHECK)**

Land a legacy brand. **(CHECK)**

Work with multiple Fortune 500 companies. **(CHECK)**

Promote the work of female directors. **(CHECK)**

$1 million in the bank! **(CHECK)**

Get acquired. **(CHECK)**

Win a Cannes Lion, aka the Oscar of the ad world.
**(GOT SHORTLISTED BUT DIDN'T GET THE HARDWARE.
BUT THE GAME AIN'T OVER.)**

Of course, none of this success came easy. There were a lot of late nights. A lot of hustle and flow, sweat and tears. As we say, nothing great is ever easy. But when you adopt the Long Game mentality, you become grateful to yourself for all the sacrifices you made. And you're able to appreciate—and even celebrate—your success in a more joyful and lasting way.

That's how it was for Antoinette, too. One morning in April 2008, after she'd been at Tyra for about eighteen months, she was holed up in her office, working on the next episode on Summer Must-Haves, her TV tuned into ABC, with the volume on low. The Emmy nominations were being announced on *The View*, so all the producers were in their offices, trying (or pretending) to work, but all eyes kept creeping back to the TV. And that's when it came: *The Tyra Banks Show* was nominated!

Antoinette started pounding on the paper-thin office wall. "Heather," she yelled. "Heather! Are you hearing this?" Right away, Heather, a fellow producer and Antoinette's best friend at the show, started pounding back. Others joined in, and pretty soon all you could hear was a low and steady thump, like thunder after a lightning strike. And then it stopped. Everyone ran out of their offices, and now all the producers—usually so cool and composed—were shouting and jumping up and down.

But that celebratory moment was nothing compared to what happened at the glamorous ceremony in L.A. in June. *The Tyra Banks Show* had a few tables, and everyone showed up looking giddy and glitzy. When they announced that Tyra had won for Outstanding Talk Show/Informative (!), coolness and composure went totally out the window as the whole team went snaking through the tables, practically high-fiving their way to the stage as applause rose up to the rafters.

When Tyra gave her speech, all Antoinette could hear was her heart pumping in her chest. *This was it!* She couldn't stop smiling, and inside she was crying—tears of joy. She was so happy. *This was why she had slept on Brillo-pad floors and sacrificed weekend after weekend and worked so damn hard on all the details.* Antoinette was holding hands with her producer-friend Winnie, and it seemed like Winnie's grip was all that tethered her to the ground, stopping her from floating away. After they got off stage, everyone was screaming, jumping up and down—no one could contain the excitement. It was a magical night, and it confirmed for Antoinette that she had chosen the right career and made the right choices along the way. And it reminded her that she was pretty damn proud and honored to be able to do her job. The best part? Antoinette had just turned thirty-two. She had reached her goal, ahead of schedule! She had the Emmy!

Antoinette knew she was never going to forget that night as long as she lived, and all the more so because she'd spent so many late, late nights working to get here. Because here's the thing: the more you play the Long Game, the quicker you'll discover that it's not so much *what* you do that brings you happiness or fulfillment, it's doing whatever you do with confidence and creativity. Remember: **you will not always be doing what you love, but you can love how you're doing it.** And the harder you work to attain your Big Dream, the sweeter that success tastes once you attain it. And you will. That's what puts the Boss in Boss Lady.

The beauty of the Long Game is that it never really ends. It's all about how you play the game with style and substance, how you rock and roll with it, bob and weave, fall and get back up. It's how you keep on hustling. Once Antoinette got her Emmys, she didn't throw in the towel and move to a yurt in the woods to contemplate the nature of the universe. And once Tricia successfully ran and sold her first business, she didn't rest on her laurels and take up knitting to pass the time. There was still work to be done, still more White Space to discover and plant flags in! Boss Ladies don't have time to kick back, relax, and coast on past successes. You gotta keep moving forward to your future glory.

But the other beautiful thing about the Long Game is that once you start playing it, it's not so hard to change up the specific game if you decide to make a mid-career or quarter-career pivot. And if you don't know *exactly* what you want to do right now, that's okay. But once you've started thinking about your next move and the move after it, you start to visualize a long-term path to success. That's translatable. It's all about experience and exposure. As we always say: never stop learning! You can apply whatever you've learned plotting your path in one profession to another profession. Once you've learned how to play the Long Game and navigate toward a North Star, you'll be even better equipped to hit the ground running if you decide to make a pivot.

The point is, you don't need to have exited the birth canal knowing exactly how you'll unleash your talents on the world. Far from it. That might be what the Status Quo would like you to believe, but the truth is, genius develops and matures in different people at different times. Contrary to popular belief, genius rarely springs from one lone computer nerd's brain in a garage in Menlo Park (although that happened once, sort of).

All women of greatness—Boss Ladies—discover and master their superpowers in different ways. As Shakespeare's sister might've said: "Some women are born great, some women achieve greatness, and some women have greatness thrust upon them." To see what we mean, let's take a look at how some of our favorite Boss Ladies in the field of entertainment worked their magic and mojo to rise up and get things done.

Use What You're Given to Get What You Want

Some of us have this feeling in us—deep down—that's been there as long as we can remember. It's the knowledge that we have this power inside us: we know what we're good at and what we want to be. It's just a question of combining our skills and our passions and doubling down on our uniqueness. This is how it was for the inimitable Lena Waithe, who, in 2017, became the first black woman to win an Emmy Award for Best Comedy Writing for the hit Netflix show *Master of None.* Lena was determined to live her dream from a young age.

"I was sort of a weirdo," she says, "because when I was seven I realized I wanted to be a television writer. I watched a ton of TV because I was raised by a single mom and spent a lot of time with my grandmother. Like most grandparents do, she would spend hours and hours in front of the TV box. I also loved spending time reading and writing, so when it came time to really figure out what I wanted to do, I put those two loves together and my family was very supportive. They were like, *Okay, this is cool. You're not pregnant, you're just going to go write TV.*"

Lena took all those hours spent watching TV with her grandmother and combined that knowledge with one of her budding skills, writing. She got a great education in TV without even knowing it and worked hard at her writing so that when she grew up those early passions helped light her way forward. It wasn't easy, of course. Lena worked for years writing for TV shows that didn't feel true to what she knew. Then, finally, one day, she found a show that was. As Lena says, "The reason I get so excited about *Master of None* is because it's showing people of color as regular people. No one is getting shot. Nobody is shooting up. I'm not a rapper. You know, my job on the show is a theater critic."

Lena embodies a key lesson: **use what you're given to get what you want.** Lena utilized the experiences that made her unique, and she doubled down on her superpowers, her humor and her writing. When Lena accepted her Emmy, she said from behind the podium: "I see each and every one of you. The things that make us different, those are our superpowers. Every day when you walk out the door, put on your imaginary cape and go out there and conquer the world because the world would not be as beautiful as it is without us in it."

Lena applied her passions to opportunities and had the confidence to keep going when it was tough because she was coming from a place of strength. Her commitment to herself and her craft, drawing on what she was given, has led her to become a beacon to aspiring LGBTQ and brown writers the world over.

Whether you're aware of it or not, you too have unique skills and passions that have shaped who you are. You just need to listen to yourself and your story so you can identify them—then figure out how you can put them to work.

Always Turn a Weakness into a Strength

Not all of us have as clear a sense of where we're headed as Lena did. Life is hard, and sometimes circumstances get in the way of our discovering our superpowers and using them to the max. But sometimes it's the very things that appear to keep us stuck that will ultimately set us free.

Take Tiffany Haddish. Tiffany became a household name after starring in the mega hit *Girls Trip,* but she'd been making people laugh for years as an actress and a stand-up comedian. In fact, she'd been cracking people up long before that, just without getting paid for it. She'd had it tough, growing up in one of the most broke neighborhoods in Los Angeles, living in foster homes, and taking care of her siblings after her mom got into a car accident.

In ninth grade, she enrolled in an all-white high school in the neighborhood of Woodland Hills. Tiffany felt like an outsider and was always getting into trouble because she didn't know any other way to make friends. "I had never been around this many white people," she remembers. "I thought I was at the Nickelodeon Awards every day, so I thought I needed to be all creative and entertaining because I thought white people lived in TV—my concept of people was really messed up."

By the time she got to tenth grade, Tiffany's social worker was getting called to the school every week. "I was getting sent to the dean's office for being racist because I had this bird named Cracker. It was this imaginary bird, and I would be like, *Cracker want a Polly?* And I would take actual crackers and break them up on my shoulder. Kids would laugh and stuff. We'd be taking a test and I would be like, *What's the answer to number seven, Cracker?* And they'd be like, *Go to the dean's office!* So my social worker was like, *You have two choices this time. You can go to Laugh Factory Academy Camp or you can go to psychiatric therapy. Which one you want to do this summer?* I was like, *Which one got drugs?* and I went to comedy camp."

That's when things changed for Tiffany. That summer, she learned a lot about comedy, of course—essential skills like how to write and how to have stage presence—but she also learned confidence, communication, and self-awareness. She finally found a place where her humor could be utilized and appreciated. Now that she knew she was *good at being funny,* she kept at it, and over time she was able to turn a defense mechanism into her greatest offensive weapon.

What Tiffany's story tells us is this: **always turn a weakness into strength.** Tiffany took her hardscrabble youth and turned it into comedy, the most generous act possible. She wrung laughter out of what had once been tears, and today Tiffany is killing it as one of the funniest motherfucking comedians on the planet.

Sometimes, the superpowers that make us stand out are the same ones that can get us into trouble. But if we work to harness them and wield them wisely, they will take us to the moon. We know you too have things in your life that have held you back—maybe you lost someone close to you, maybe you didn't have a ton of friends as a kid, maybe you didn't grow up in the right zip code. All that's in the past now; but you can still turn that past into a brighter future. Remember that success starts with strength, and nothing makes you stronger than surviving and thriving despite all the setbacks. That's power!

Knowledge Knows No Boundaries

Some of us don't discover our truest talents till later in life. Sometimes we spend years working in one area only to realize that our true talents would be better applied elsewhere. The key is to trust yourself enough to know that it's never too late to change the direction of your life and the trajectory of your future.

Once, there was a young brown woman who began her career as a film publicist, and she was damn good at it. She became a fierce advocate for her clients, starting her own firm after only four years. But she couldn't seem to shake that nagging feeling that something was missing. One day, she had an epiphany. She loved spending time with film directors but had never believed that she had what it took to become one of them. Until, suddenly, it dawned on her. "*They're just regular people, like me, with ideas,*" she thought to herself. "*I've got ideas.*" "That's literally how it all started," she recalled. "It was definitely a career change; I didn't make my first little short until I was thirty-two.... But I did start to recognize that being so close to really great filmmakers and watching them direct on set and the experiences that I did have, although different from film school, were still super valuable. I learned just from being around. I coupled that with some very intentional study and practice—picking up a camera—and started just making it."

At thirty-two, she made her first short film. Up until then, she'd assumed that directing was something she couldn't do. It wasn't until she finally realized the people she was working with were just like her that she was able to kick the self-doubt and find the courage to go after her dream. After fourteen years as a publicist, she quit and used $50,000 from her personal savings to finance her first feature film.

The woman's name is Ava DuVernay, and she went on to direct *Selma*, which was nominated for Best Picture, and a documentary about mass incarceration called *13th* that also got nods from the Academy. Now she's one of the most sought-after directors in Hollywood.

Ava didn't know what she wanted to do from Day One (or Two or Three), but over time she realized that she had powers and passions within her that weren't finding the fullest expression. All superpowers take time to master. You should be open to the idea that the thing you thought you "wanted to be when you grew up" might have been the first thing that allowed you to express some of your talent and power, but it doesn't have to be the only thing.

The truth is we all have a far broader range of options than we are aware of. Let's say you've dreamed of becoming an actress for most of your life. What are the essential strengths and passions you're tapping into when you act? If what you really love about acting is giving hope to people by performing, and bringing stories to life, there's a good chance you'd also make a terrific social worker, or drama teacher, or nurse at a children's hospital. Keep returning to your strength and your superpower, and the truth of your purpose will reveal itself. You'll be able to take all you've already learned with you into your next phase, and you'll be stronger for it. You don't have to follow anyone else's script. As we always say: **a Boss Lady doesn't follow fashions, she leads them.**

On the Download

Where you are today isn't where you'll be tomorrow.
It's like the old saying *Don't dress for the job you have, dress for the job you want.* Adopt the Long Game mentality and know that you're going places. It's a simple trick, but just knowing where you're going will get you there faster.

You can't rely on wishful thinking, you have to rely on listful thinking.
Put your plans and dreams down on paper to make yourself accountable.

The Long Game is about you, not anyone else.
It can be tempting to compare yourself to the people around you, but remember, you're headed to your North Star, not theirs. When you get distracted by everyone around you, that's when the Status Quo pulls ahead and wins.

The only way you'll get where you want to go is by relentlessly believing you'll get there.
You'll achieve success on your terms only by doubling down on yourself again and again. Most people are too scared to state their dreams. Boss Ladies aren't most people. Double down on your dreams and start planning how to get there.

Know your future prize—and double down on getting it.
Don't get distracted by short-term rewards or incentives; they will only derail you from your path. Stay focused on attaining your Big Dream, and make choices that bring you closer to attaining it.

The higher you aim, the higher you'll rise.
No one ever became the best at anything by telling themselves they wanted to be mediocre. You need to be bold and ambitious in what you want to accomplish, and your work ethic will follow suit.

You will not always be doing what you love, but you can love how you're doing it.

When you play the Long Game, there are no shortcuts. There'll be times when you're doing work that is (1) hard and yet (2) beneath you. But the harder the work, the more you'll enjoy and appreciate your successes. True pleasure comes from executing quality work, no matter what the work is.

Use what you're given to get what you want.

You may not choose your superpower, but it's what you've got and it's going to get you where you need to go.

Always turn a weakness into a strength.

We all have flaws that sometimes get us into trouble. But when we wield them wisely, they will set us free.

Knowledge knows no boundaries.

It's never too late to follow a new passion, hone a new skill, or discover a new superpower. Take what you already know and apply it to where you want to go.

chapter four

Don't Hedge Your Bets, Take the Risk

No one doubles down harder than Mom. When there's a problem, she'll solve it. If she's jammed up, she'll break free. If it's raining and she doesn't have an umbrella, she'll design one on a napkin, construct it from scratch, and then walk all around town with it, singin' in the rain. She refuses to let anyone else be the author of her destiny. She'll write that shit herself, thank you very much. Mom stays steady when the rest of the world is roiling.

When things get tough, Mom just gets tougher.

When we were little, Mom ran her single-parent household and twin-child duties while also working a demanding full-time job. She carefully hoarded her sick days and vacation time so she could be with us if *we* were sick or *we* had a school vacation. And when she couldn't be in two places at once—though if *anyone could* be in two places at once, it'd be Mom—she enlisted the help of the Fam. They were only too happy to help since that's just how we all roll—that love is deep and dedicated. We're thicker than thieves and more opinionated than Fox News (only, the opposite opinions). Everyone pitched in to help when they could.

One rare weekend when we were eight years old, the two of us went out to Long Island to hang with Aunt Monica. Mom was pumped because it meant that she had two whole days to herself. We were pumped because usually we spent parts of our weekends with Grandma (on Turner Place) or Aunt Leonie (one block away), but this time, *we got to go to the burbs*. We know . . . the grass is always greener on the other side of the fence. But the grass is *for real* the greenest in the suburbs. We used to dream of living out in the burbs because that's the image of life we saw on TV. White fences, white neighbors, and lots of hamburgers sizzling on red Black & Decker grills.

Aunt Monica was no-nonsense. She had no choice. As the head of her own construction company, she had to play rough with the big boys (recalcitrant foreman, tough unions) on the regular. She knew how to dial it back at home—a little—but still, she suffered no fools. She ran a tight ship, especially in the kitchen, where she loved to make sweets. This worked out well for us, because we loved to eat sweets. She baked cakes, cookies, cupcakes—and our favorite treat at the time: a pink Jell-O pie with a thick crust that she called Dream Pie. (It turns our stomach now, just thinking about it, but that sugar bomb used to be the light of our lives.)

Another thing that Aunt Monica knew how to do was hair. She could braid hair like a veteran hairdresser at the corner salon—the one with a line coming out the door. Mom always did our hair in boring pigtails or a ponytail—and always the same for both of us—so we were *super* excited to get our hair done at Monica's.

In short, we had big plans for the weekend; we were gonna go wild.

Saturday morning we were living the suburban dream, chilling in the backyard—that green grass, that white fence—Tricia getting her do done and Antoinette running around like a maniac, occasionally stopping only to sneak finger-scoops of leftover chocolate frosting while Aunt Monica, who had her scrunched-up concentration face turned toward Tricia's hair, wasn't watching. Antoinette wasn't supposed to run much on account of her horrible asthma, but that frosting had given her a rocket boost of energy. It was a vicious, sugar-fueled cycle. Then the crash came.

When it was finally Antoinette's turn to get braided—while Tricia marveled at her new look in the reflection of the pool—Aunt Monica noticed pretty quickly that Antoinette sounded funny. Not like ha-ha funny, but like *irregular and something's up* funny. So she gave Antoinette a hit off her asthma inhaler, but it didn't help. If anything, Antoinette was wheezing harder and harder and her chest was getting tighter and tighter, like there was a boa constrictor around her chest. Antoinette's mind was flooded with fear and panic. She. Couldn't. Breathe. Aunt Monica tried the "rescue inhaler," and then, when even that didn't help, she ran into the house and got out the Nebulizer—an oxygen mask that sends medicine into the lungs even faster. But still Antoinette couldn't catch her breath. This was bad. Aunt Monica called Mom, told her what was up and what was about to go down: she was taking Antoinette to the ER. So we all piled into Aunt Monica's beige Buick Regal and booked it to Brookhaven Memorial Hospital.

Now, Antoinette was severely asthmatic, so an attack was not at all out of the ordinary. In fact, we used to joke about how at any family gathering there was a good chance there'd be at least one catch-your-breath scare. But this one was off the charts. It wasn't a 10, it was an 11. Obviously, Mom rushed out to the hospital and made it from Brooklyn in record time. Meanwhile, things were getting worse, to the point where eventually they had to put Antoinette on an oxygen tank. Where she stayed through Sunday. Then Monday.

Then Tuesday, Wednesday, Thursday, Friday.

Mom was there at the hospital the whole time. She was almost as sick as Antoinette with all her worry. And she was worried about Tricia, who at this point was scared as hell. But Mom was also worried she was going to lose her job. She'd already used up her sick days and vacation. She knew this was a legit emergency, but she also knew that some people at work might not be so sympathetic to a single mom who misses so much work. She worried that she wouldn't be believed.

Mom made sure to keep her boss, Mr. Shazzad, up-to-date on what was going on. Despite how freaked out she was feeling inside, she stayed calm and collected as she tried to make him understand why she had no choice other than to stay with Antoinette. After a week of missing work, she called him and said, "I know I'm missing a lot of work, but you can come to see for yourself how bad things are. It's Brookhaven Memorial." No tears, no pity party. Just the facts. Then she got off the phone and went back to be with Antoinette.

On Monday morning, when Mom was down the hall talking with some nurses, Antoinette woke up to see a strange man in a suit standing in the middle of her room.

NETTE

Who are you?

STRANGE MAN IN A SUIT

I'm Mr. Shazzad. I work with your mom.

NETTE

You're the man on the telephone?
The boss-man?

MR. SHAZZAD
(FORMERLY KNOWN AS STRANGE MAN IN A SUIT)

That's me. How're you feeling?

NETTE

Not great.

Mom came back into the room and was as shocked as Antoinette to see him. She hadn't thought that Mr. Shazzad would *actually* come out to Long Island to see for himself, but he had. And not because he wanted to make sure that her story checked out; he came out to see if there was anything he could do. He had two kids, too, and Mom had got him thinking of how he'd feel if one of his kids was sick.

Thankfully, in the end, Mom didn't lose Antoinette (obviously!)— or her job. After two weeks in the hospital, Antoinette was released, good as new. What would come to be known as the severest asthma incident in Our History was over.

And Tricia still had her cute braids.

Obviously, we were too young for this to register at the time, but looking back we've always wondered how Mom managed to keep her shit on lock even when it seemed like everything was coming apart. She did what needed to be done, and she kept her cool while doing it. Even as her daughter lay there hooked up to a tank of oxygen, she was able to embody grace under pressure. She could have given in to the fear. She could've broken down and lost faith. But she knew she had to have faith for the three of us. Mom was a Boss Lady. To this day, whenever we feel on the verge of breaking down, of losing faith, or when we're encountering a big obstacle, we try to keep calm and collected the way Mom did for those two weeks. And that's how we know we have the strength to handle whatever shit comes our way.

When the Going Gets Tough

Shit happens to all of us at some point in our lives. It doesn't matter if you're rich or poor, if you live in the suburbs or the city, if you're married, single, or a single mom of twins, shit happens. And when it does, you have two choices. You can let fear break you, or you can rise above it. **When the going gets tough, you just need to get tougher.**

This chapter is about how, at the exact moment you feel the most defeated, deflated, or denied, and all you want to do is crawl under your desk or your duvet, you need to take a deep breath and tell yourself: "*I got this!*" It's time to be bold and confident despite the odds.

As human beings, we're wired to fear fear—and so we try to avoid the feelings associated with it. That sinking feeling in the pit of your stomach, that quickened beating of your heart, and the dreaded upper-lip sweat—that's what fear feels like. And it's paralyzing.

But fear is also unavoidable. It's one of the few things in life that none of us can get around. Fear of the unknown. Fear of failing. Fear of not being good enough.

But it's also fear of your own power. Your own prowess. Your own audacity. And that is fear's most pernicious quality—it gets inside your head, and little by little it begins to eat away at your confidence, and your belief in your superpower. Fear can make you hate what you love.

In a way, fear is like a hangover: your head hurts, your eyes itch; you're cranky and hungry (but also nauseous); you're too wired to go back to sleep but too tired to stay awake. There's only one thing you can commit to doing: nothing.

It's the same when you're hustling and trying to change the world. You'll encounter setbacks that'll leave you confused, disoriented, un-motivated. Because that's what the Status Quo wants. The Status Quo wants you to be nervous, to question yourself, to second-guess your worth, to downplay your power, and to shut down. The Status Quo wants you to stay on that couch in those dirty leggings, binge-watching the latest Netflix show. F that! You should be getting off the couch and *running the show*!

We want you to embrace the fear, along with your own audac-ity. We want you to pick yourself up and keep going. We want you to keep putting yourself on the line. We want you to face the terror—and the upper-lip sweat and the stomach butterflies. That fear is power—raw—waiting to be converted into success. You can refine fear into energy to move you forward.

Because here's the thing: **the only way to truly fail is by failing to try.** Most people never try—not really. They play it safe. They listen, follow the rules, work inside the box, paint by numbers—all that Bullshit Status Quo stuff. But what they don't realize is that taking risks—actually *doing* something that scares you, something you've never done before—that's what makes it fun to be alive.

Without risk, we'd be nowhere. Human beings would all still be sitting cold and hungry in a field, wishing we knew what the hell was going on and what we were supposed to do about it. Instead, our ancestors got up, gave birth, made tools, foraged for food, discovered fire, grafted plants, hunted animals, built railroads, invented electricity, climbed mountains, sailed seas, even went to the moon and back. Plus, humans invented chocolate chip cookie dough ice cream! So you see, without risk, there's no reward. Life doesn't just hand out fat checks to people for no reason. Just as in blackjack, you have to bet big if you want to win big. You have to put yourself out there—again and again—to get the recognition you deserve.

There are two types of people in this world: the people who sit back waiting for things to happen *to* them, and the people who take a risk and make things happen *for* them.

You are the second kind of person.

When you go big, is there a chance you will totally miss the mark? Sure. But you're still in a better position than before you tried—even if you feel blue as hell. Because when you take a chance and fail, what's left is information. What's left is learning. That's what you gotta keep in mind.

That learning comes in two forms: (1) as bankable knowledge about how you've miscalculated and how you can change your approach; or (2) as evidence that the Status Quo is up in your shit and you've got to persist anyway—because you believe in yourself and your idea and you are going to keep on hustling and proving yourself to the world!

Again as in blackjack: you gotta know when to hold 'em and when to fold 'em. See, you're not usually gonna get dealt winning cards every hand. And if you stick around at the table for long enough, you're gonna lose some hands. But you need to keep things in perspective and keep playing that Long Game. You might have to change up your approach, but you don't go giving up everything because you experience a few setbacks. Failure is a chance to take an honest look at what's going on and decide whether to fold, keep your eyes on the dealer, and tweak your strategy for the next hand, or whether to stay in, double down, and refuse to let the Status Quo fuck with your thinking.

Everyone feels fear, and everyone experiences failure. What matters isn't whether you feel fear but whether you keep calm and carry on. What matters isn't whether you failed yesterday but how quickly you'll bounce back tomorrow. Only Boss Ladies know that you have to be willing to chance it, work it, and come back the next day ready to give it your all.

Back in 1980 there was an aspiring female musician looking to make her mark in the world of rock 'n' roll. She recorded a tape with two songs on it and sent it to twenty-three record companies—and got rejected by all of them. Can you imagine getting the fifteenth, let alone the twenty-third, rejection letter? Soul crushing! But do you think she threw in the towel? Did she sell her guitar, get a haircut and a blowout, and decide to become a secretary at the local bank branch? Did she think to herself, *Well, I guess they're right. I'm not cut out to be a rock star. Time to get a steady paycheck. I guess I don't really love rock 'n' roll after all?*

Hell no! Boss Ladies don't quit—they double down. They don't conform to the odds, they defy them. This aspiring rock star went all-in on her skills and went out to make shit happen: she started her own label. Her self-titled debut album sold so well that, wouldn't you know, one of those twenty-three record labels came knocking and offered to rerelease it. And then, later that year, she made her second album. It was called *I Love Rock 'n' Roll*—named after one of the tracks on the original tape she'd sent out. The album went on to sell ten million copies. The musician's name was Joan Jett.

It would've been really easy for Boss Lady Joan Jett to interpret all twenty-three rejections as evidence her music wasn't up to snuff. But she *knew* that she had talent to unleash upon the world. She held strong, and it paid off big time. "Don't listen to the so-called experts," she once said. ". . . If you think you've got what it takes and really believe in yourself and you're ready to take a lot of crap and still want to do it, go for it."

You can't let early hardship prevent you from pursuing your dreams. Take it from our dear friend and another Boss Lady, Loren Ridinger, who cofounded Market America/Shop.com with her husband, JR, in 1992. When we spoke with Loren, she recalled, "Twenty-six years ago nobody thought people would shop online. It was really JR's vision that one day people would shop online. People thought he was crazy because they were so used to touching and trying on products. Plus people didn't even have computers back then. Trying to convince people to change their habits was hard!" But JR, Loren, and Loren's brother, Mark, believed in the vision. They knew they weren't crazy! Loren says, "We stayed up until 3 a.m. Two computers

working in our house, we didn't have an office. We had every reason in the world to quit. There was no money, no salaries—tacos at
Wendy's Super Bar. That was our big dinner. We went days without
a solid meal; there was no way to hire someone to help." And if that
all wasn't stressful enough, the year that Market America started was
the year Loren's mom died and the year she gave birth to her daughter. And to boot, Loren was only twenty-one years old, without a clue
how to juggle it all. She couldn't afford day care, so it was Take Your
Daughter to Work Day—every day. But the three of them (well, now
four, with the baby) stuck it out—because they wanted to change
things, and they believed in their mission.

As we always say: nothing great is easy.

Go Big or Go Home

We've always wanted to make an impact, a splash, an impression.
Ever since we were little, we've been obsessed with doing things differently; we get easily bored with the same-old, same-old. Like the
time Aunt Monica gave us a cookbook for kids—all very simple reci-
pes, including one for cookies. We were into it—obviously—but we
soon wanted to go bigger. We didn't just want to bake cookies like
everyone else, we wanted to make something *special* . . . like candy!
Obviously neither of us had a clue how to do this, so we started experimenting. We were like a pair of wild-eyed bakers, running madly
about the kitchen putting our sugary concoctions in the oven and
then in the fridge and then back in the oven until we got it to just
the right consistency. And bam, we had taffy! Mom thought we were
crazy. We thought it was delicious!

We've lived by the following philosophy ever since: with big risks
come big rewards. And nothing tastes sweeter than the candy you
make yourself! At different points in our lives, we've both stared

down our fear, followed our guts despite conventional wisdom, and wholly embraced the uncertainty that precedes change.

Tricia's biggest professional gamble was when she left a successful career and a good salary at Emmis—a venerable, traditional media company—and went to work for Global Grind, a start-up that was going through some pretty big growing pains. Leaving a comfortable corporate job at a company she loved—and where she'd spent much of her career—was difficult. Tricia knew she'd face some serious challenges, but she also knew that she would profit from overcoming them. Tricia believed she had the skills to turn the company around—and she knew that working in that kind of environment, with that kind of increased responsibility, would bring her closer to her dream of starting her own company, being her own boss, and working with people she respected to bring about change in her industry.

She was also taking a sizable pay cut, but the offer came with equity—the very definition of risky! If her efforts were successful, her stake in it could someday be worth serious money. But if they failed, well, her shares could be worth next to nothing. Tricia was betting on the company's success, sure, but she was also betting on herself. She was betting that she'd be able to do what the job demanded. She was betting that her extensive experience had prepared her for this new challenge. She was doubling down.

It wasn't always smooth sailing, not by a long shot, but ultimately that leap into the unknown turned out to be the best decision of her life. If she hadn't made that decision, if she hadn't taken that chance, she never would've created Narrative_, which turned out to be her dream all along.

There are Decisive Moments in everyone's life when you can choose to be either a Passenger or a Pilot. This was one of those Decisive Moments for Tricia. And that's how she looked at it. She could have continued coasting along, leading the digital division at Emmis but still hampered by the company's size and bureaucracy, or she could take the wheel, actively leading the charge.

Deciding to change jobs, as Tricia did, or maybe even to change professions entirely, is *super* intimidating. Maybe you're in the thick of it right now. You've been working as an administrative assistant, but you decide you want to go to nursing school. You've been teaching high school, but you realize you want to be an actor. You've been working in HR, but you realize you want to get an MBA. Or like Ava DuVernay, you've been working as a film publicist, but you realize you want to direct. These are those Decisive Moments. If you've been doing the work, you'll know what to do: **at a Decisive Moment, go all-in.** This is when you'll need to pull a Stevie Nicks and go your own way.

One Boss Lady who's gone her own way, taken big risks, weathered storms, and stayed true to her abiding passions is Anne Wojcicki, the CEO and cofounder of 23andMe, whom we mentioned in chapter 2.

Anne was always interested in the human body and health care. "As a child," she told us when we spoke to her, "I loved my pediatrician. I loved the hospital system. I loved how interesting it all was." She couldn't hide her excitement and passion for how miraculous the human body is: "There's this amazing machinery in your body! And that it knows what to do! It's amazing! It's the ultimate engineering project." She knew she eventually wanted a career that combined her passion for health and science, so right after college she took a job investing in health care and biotech. Anne worked on Wall Street for ten years, learning all she could about the financial side, before she finally saw an opportunity to enact real change in a flawed system, and started her own company.

Anne saw that the power of the genomic revolution—the race

to map the human genome—combined with the power of crowd-sourced genetic knowledge could offer a new way of approaching disease prevention and treatment. But rather than creating more go-betweens distancing a patient from a doctor, or a patient from his or her health information, Anne decided to put the patient in the driver's seat. She founded 23andMe in 2006 and launched the first product in 2007, with the goal of giving people—not doctors—the tools to understand their unique DNA and empowering consumers to take charge of their own health. It was a bold move, and incredibly exciting! But it didn't take off right away.

In the beginning, Anne says, "we were selling fifteen to twenty kits a day. It wasn't made for the masses. The only thing you do with that is learn. Every day is a learning opportunity. The only way that you learn is by getting feedback."

Anne and her team kept trying to refine their message to communicate the great need for and benefits of their product—and to assure people that (a) their medical data would be kept private and (b) they could trust in the accuracy of their test results. Back then, there were a lot of doubters; for a brief time the FDA questioned their methods and was skeptical whether ordinary folks would be able to understand and interpret their results without a doctor's involvement. Instead of viewing this slow start as an omen that her idea would fail, Anne viewed it as part of the long process of trial and error, of learning.

To her, it never felt like the response was a failure. "It was like, *We have to make some adjustments*. Which is a really different mind-set. We *have to change some things*. It's the scientific mind-set. *We gotta learn!* It's never been done before."

"If you keep yourself focused on the long run," she told us, "there's nothing really that's a failure."

So Anne kept at it. She was playing the Long Game. She gave hundreds of talks around the country to raise awareness about the benefit of a crowdsourced bank of information on how our genetic makeup affects our health. In the process, she discovered that people loved another feature of the product: Beyond what our DNA tells us about our health, it also holds the keys to our ancestry. People loved learning about their lineage, where their ancestors came from, to help them see a clearer picture of who they were. And that helped drive people to the product, which expanded the bank of available information, thus making the data that much more reliable. Anne also worked closely with the FDA to ensure the product met its regulatory standards. It should go without saying that ignoring the laws and regulations is the one kind of risk you *don't* want to take. So Anne didn't.

Through it all, Anne never lost faith in her core mission that if you can empower people and educate them, you can help them become more conscientious about their health—in the long run saving on costs and prolonging healthy lives. She encountered plenty of obstacles on the way, but she's been able to raise over $480 million in venture capital to fund her dream. She embodies the philosophy *go big or go home.* She never gave up and she never gave in.

We don't want you to ever give up or give in either. If you have an idea, a passion, and a purpose—one that you believe in with every fiber of your being—you need to go all-in. You need to bet on yourself and refuse to let the Status Quo win.

Know When to Hold

The Status Quo can get the better of any of us if we're not careful. It can get inside our heads, cloud our thinking, and make us think that up is down and left is right. That's the thing about the Status Quo: it can make you think you're working hard to get what you want, personally and professionally, when really you're working double time to undermine yourself. This happens when you let the Status Quo dictate your destiny.

Some years ago, Antoinette was flying high. She and her production team had recently won two Emmys for their work on *The Tyra Banks Show* and she'd just moved into an apartment in a brownstone with her boyfriend at the time. They'd been dating for a year and a half. Tricia was already married, and at thirty-four Antoinette felt like she needed to follow suit. Some of her friends were even having kids, and they started asking her, the way your friends with kids always do, "When are you and _____ gonna settle down?" Of course, what they really mean is, "When are you and _____ gonna, settle down and have kids . . . just like us?"

Antoinette felt pressure on the relationship, from inside and out. She was constantly asking herself, *Where is this going? What's the next step? When is he going to put a ring on it?* The problem was she was so focused on the future, she wasn't paying attention to what was happening in the here and now.

One day, she came home and found his open laptop on the table. Never one to snoop, Antoinette was surprised when she felt an overpowering urge to take just a little peek. You know where this is going: straight to a nonplatonic e-mail thread with an ex-girlfriend.

Antoinette was devastated. She did *not* see this one coming. She felt kind of the same way she did that fateful Saturday at Aunt Monica's: short of breath, like the wind had been knocked right out of her. Antoinette laid into her (now ex-) boyfriend with some righteous anger and then called Tricia in tears, frantically packing socks into a Goyard bag.

NETTE
I just need to pack up some clothes and I'm
walking out the door.

TRISH
Clothes? WE ARE THE SAME SIZE. FUCKING LEAVE!

The next day was the first time in five years Antoinette had missed a day of work. She was a mess. But in hindsight she realized she was less upset about the loss of the boyfriend per se than about the loss of the future—husband, two kids, house in the burbs—that the Status Quo (and all her married friends) *thought she should want to have.*

After a few days, she was ready to go back to work, and when she showed up for the morning's all-staff meeting, there was only one item on that day's agenda.

1. Show's canceled.

Within a few weeks, she had lost the love of her life (she thought), another job (thanks to the unpredictable nature of TV production), and her favorite apartment ever. She'd given up her studio with floor-to-ceiling built-in bookcases on Fifteenth Street and Fifth Avenue to move in with this man! Cruel fate!

Antoinette's confidence was at an all-time low. Luckily, she at least had Tricia's guest bedroom to camp out in. After three days of moping Antoinette said, "Enough of this wallowing!" She called a real-estate broker. The bottom had fallen out from under her, but she wasn't going to be hobbled by this massive setback. She acted quickly to implement pragmatic solutions. She activated her squad and put out feelers for producing jobs.

When the going gets tough, you need to get tougher.

Antoinette got an interview for a job at *The Nate Berkus Show,* which was just starting production and hadn't aired its first show. On the morning of the interview, she was *tired*: she'd stayed up the whole night, prepping and trying to find something really unique to pitch that she thought Nate would dig.

But a few minutes into the interview, Antoinette decided to ditch the canned ideas she'd come up with and just lead with what was real to her. So she pitched a segment about women starting over or moving on after a breakup. She suggested calling it "The Next Chapter."

Two weeks later, Antoinette's phone rang: she had gotten the job! The breakup still stung (and so did the whole finding-a-new-apartment thing), but her career was back on track. And at least she'd come away with a valuable lesson: she'd let the Status Quo get up inside her head, and as a result she'd put too much pressure on herself, and on the relationship. She'd been so preoccupied with where they were going that she couldn't see where they were, and she'd been much too quick to decide they were ready to move into his apartment together. But she took solace in the fact that in the end, when shit went down, she had refused to fold. She gave herself time to wallow, and then she got down to biz. She was bouncing back and moving forward, confidently, with her New Chapter.

As we said, the Status Quo can get the better of any of us if we let it. It got inside Tricia's head—albeit in a different form—once she'd successfully launched Narrative_. The Status Quo can lure you away from your true intentions in all sorts of ways.

Narrative_ was always a scrappy enterprise. That was its virtue and its purpose. It was an agency but it was also an innovation lab, focusing on code and culture—leveraging tech to move a story forward and culture to help ID the stories Narrative_ wanted to tell. It was a place where all ideas were concepted and tested, which meant it could take chances that bigger, less nimble agencies couldn't or didn't care to. The first year Narrative_ was in business, Tricia secured amazing clients. The second year in business, she doubled revenue.

Then Tricia started feeling pressure to increase the company's exposure and win more business. To get more respect from the industry and land bigger clients, she decided they needed some industry cred. That is, Narrative_ was going to have to win some big awards. The more the better: *a Clio, a Cannes Lion, a Shorty, a Webby, a One Show, an AICP.* She thought to herself: *The big agencies have these awards and people take them so seriously. I need to win some of these accolades!*

Since creative acumen drives an agency's reputation, she figured she should get some accomplished creatives on her team. And because advertising is a bit of a Boy's Club, she decided to bring in some of the boys. The problem was that the industry insiders she hired were accustomed to multimillion-dollar campaigns with large teams, tons of support staff, freelancers, and lots of lead time to come up with creative ideas—and they didn't show much if any interest in adapting themselves to Narrative_'s leaner staff and quicker, nimbler moves. These guys had won the awards the old-fashioned way—by spending a lot of money. Narrative_ didn't have those resources.

At the big agencies they were used to, there's very little collaboration. The creatives handed down their ideas as if they were kings issuing edicts to their subjects! Tricia wanted to innovate, to use technology to tell stories, and to exploit the young staff's cultural intelligence, but every time she suggested something the high-priced talent would look at her like: "What do *you* know? You're not a creative director." They weren't interested in working with Narrative_ to come up with ideas, they were interested in Narrative_ carrying out their ideas.

Still, Tricia tried to accommodate them and give them the tools to succeed—but it wasn't translating. It got to the point where she started second-guessing her own creative instincts, thinking, *Well, maybe these guys are right. I mean, they've won awards at other agencies and they're really well respected. Maybe I should give them room to breathe and see what they come up with.* Because she respected their accomplishments, she was afraid to say no to some of their big spending and was too quick to say yes to some of their ideas. After they burned through a bunch of money—with no results to show for it—she was left holding the bag.

> TRISH
>
> Hey, so, I think I made a mistake.

> NETTE
>
> You pregnant?

> TRISH
>
> Nah. Different kind. I think I just lit a bunch of dollars on fire by paying these dudes so much money. I just did my books and I had to cut my salary in half and put a chunk of my savings into Narrative_.

> NETTE
>
> Girl, you ceded your creative power to these dudes because you thought they'd be a magic bullet. There are no magic bullets. There's only you, your team, and your dream. You gotta do things your way, the way the DNA of Narrative_ dictates, you can't try to replicate the success of others blindly. You know this!

Tricia *did* know this! She'd just let the Status Quo get in the way of her thinking. The thing is when we start doubting ourselves, straying from our ideals, and letting our fear take the front seat, we might as well hand the Status Quo the win right then and there. *Game's over, you win.* Tricia really wanted the prestige of a Cannes Lion to bolster her agency's image, and she let her desire for it—or rather her fear that Narrative_ wouldn't be taken seriously if she *didn't* get it—lead her into the morass of Bullshit Status Quo thinking. In hindsight, she realized that she'd tried to take a shortcut by outsourcing the very thing that was Narrative_'s great virtue in the marketplace: being scrappy and arriving at one-of-a-kind solutions through trial and error and experimenting.

Tricia had forgotten her Long Game. Narrative_'s strategy had never been about operating like the other guys; if it did that, it'd be out of business. But did Tricia beat herself up for her mistake or give up on her dream of winning that Lion? Hell no! She wised up, saw the experience as the learning opportunity that it was, and course-corrected. She got rid of the expensive talent and went back to hiring people whose passion was leading them to new places. She focused on coming in to work the next day, and the next day, and the next day after that, and trying again—only better. And once Tricia re-turned to the true DNA of Narrative_, day in and day out, that was when she began to attract the industry attention she'd sought origi-nally, eventually winning the awards (Clios, Webbys, Shortys) she'd wanted originally.

And that's what separates the Hustlers from the Hustled. It's never letting the Status Quo—whether it's other people or that voice in your head—define who you are, what your value is, and how you'll pursue your goals.

Know When to Fold

We both grow restless if we aren't taking risks, and that's why we've chosen to work in fields that allow for creativity and experimenta-tion. We're not averse to a little adversity, we're not overly challenged by challenges. Then again, we've been in some tough spots that have made us question ourselves and what we were doing. And what we were able to see was that the more painful or frightening the experience was, the more we actually learned from it, even if we didn't see it that way from the start.

Early on in our careers, we decided to take a risk together. This was when Antoinette wasn't making much bank as a producer and was looking for a side hustle to earn some extra dollars, while Tricia was restless at her Emmis job and wanted to sink her teeth into something new to keep her mind active. Suddenly, a problem we were both having became an opportunity.

Back then we were both working some pretty long hours, and we would often leave work at eight or nine and head directly downtown to meet our crew for dinner or to check out a club. Only we couldn't find any tops that were professional-looking enough to wear around the office and also stylish enough to take us from day into night. It was a First World problem, we recognize, but still! No matter how hard we looked, we couldn't find cool tops that would work for us uptown and downtown. Well, a problem is just an opportunity, and you know what that means—White Space! Since we both wanted more cash and credibility, we said to ourselves: *Shit, we're problem solvers. If it doesn't exist, create it.*

NETTE

You know what?

TRISH

What, girl?

NETTE

We're starting a clothing line!

And that was the birth of TAC Clothing.

Pretty quickly, we ran into our first major roadblock. And by *pretty quickly* we mean, like, immediately. The thing was, we knew literally nothing about designing clothes, finding wholesalers, cutting cloth, creating patterns, sourcing labor, or setting up accounts with distributors.

And it didn't matter, we'd learn.

We hired a sketch artist with some money we'd saved from our day jobs and told her our vision. We ran the sketches by our friends and family and used their feedback to refine our concepts. We took the subway down to New York's garment district and selected fabrics—silks, textured jersey, lace crochet—and had samples made.

If we were going to run an e-commerce business, though, we were obviously going to need a website. So we scoured the Internet for sites we thought combined class, usability, and fun and sent them to a few web designers Tricia had worked with in the past.

Then we activated our crew. A friend pitched in to take the photos for us. Another, who was the creative director at an ad agency, created our logo and the Look Book we used to display our collection. In short, we hustled the hell out of our side hustle!

We concepted it that April, and we launched in September!

We soon learned two things: the first was that women *loved* our tops. The response was incredibly validating. We found out that we could start a business from scratch and actually land ourselves in stores: in New York, L.A., and Miami. We sold out most of our inventory—hundreds of tops—proof that we had created something other women wanted, something they were willing to pay hard-earned money for—even though we weren't a well-known brand!

The other thing we learned was more sobering: just because you have a good product that people love doesn't necessarily mean you're going to be cashing checks. The thing was, 50 percent of the stores we were in didn't end up paying us because *their* businesses were struggling; since we were one of the smaller companies they bought from, we were last on their list to get paid (i.e., *not get paid at all*). It's really hard to create a fashion label! We lost every single penny we put into the business—and Trish had invested her own money.

We had to admit, we'd been naive. We'd assumed that just because we knew fashion we also knew what it took to succeed in the fashion business. We'd gone in knowing next to nothing about clothing sales, manufacturing, production, and marketing, assuming it would be as easy as when we resold those Guess sweatshirts. We'd taken a huge risk, and it hadn't gone exactly according to plan.

While we lost dollars—and damn, we wished we hadn't—we were eventually able to see our effort for what it was: an incredible education. We'd actively moved outside our comfort zone, and that fact boosted our confidence rather than diminishing it, as the Status Quo wants.

Here's another thing the Status Quo wants: it wants you to believe the myth that successful people never make mistakes, never F things up. Well, take it from us: all great works, all great inventions, all great successes are produced through trial and error, and no one gets it right on the first try, every time.

The people who are the best at their jobs, no matter what work they do, approach their craft the same way—as **problem solvers**. Every assignment, gig, or project is a new problem in need of solving. And the only way to arrive at a good, workable solution that will deliver big results is to test and prototype.

We think about our work as prototyping. Prototyping is about taking a problem, using trial and error to come up with a promising solution, and then doubling down on it. A film editor wants to make a scene crisp, clear, and exciting. So she comes up with the idea to create a seamless flow of individual shots to create the illusion of continuous action. Then she starts editing it—this angle, that cut— until finally, after constantly tweaking and trying different takes and sequences, she has what she's looking for. A wedding planner wants to create a special mood for her clients, while also working within a certain budget. So she comes up with ways to execute their vision for less money by calling different venues, price checking, and doing some things DIY. In any kind of work, any situation, prototyping means experimenting, then gathering feedback to inform your next step. When you're prototyping, you're building out your knowledge base, your skills and your experiences, actively, by doing. As we always say: never stop learning!

Ever since we were little, we've used the Prototype Mentality to test whether our ideas were on the right track—and to keep ourselves from getting too hung up on an idea that wasn't. The Prototype Mentality is a powerful—and empowering—way to look at the world because it means no options are off the table. Whether it was making taffy in our kitchen, launching a risky business venture, or taking a leap of faith in a relationship, if we tested an idea and it didn't work, either we'd refine it and try again or we'd move on to the next one. If things didn't go our way, we didn't take it as a personal failing. We were just trying shit out! And if we cut our losses and moved on, we didn't think of it as giving up. We were just choosing a new adventure.

Remember those books from when you were a kid, Choose Your Own Adventure? We loved that idea because it was our version of Mom's philosophy: be the author of your own destiny. This was the attitude that our whole family had. Take our cousin Michelle. She was the smartest of all the cousins, at least in the conventional sense. She worked super hard in high school and went to Haverford College and then straight to NYU Medical School. If you were in our family, you became either a lawyer or a doctor (before we came along and broke the mold, that is), and Michelle opted for the latter.

Thing was: she hated it. She gave med school her all for two (*loooong*) years, but she just didn't jibe with it. So she decided to see what was behind door #2. She applied to NYU law school, obviously got in, and studied like a beast. She practiced law for ten years and then she took a break to be a full-time mother. But after spending five or six years with her kids, raising them up, she knew she couldn't just hop back into practicing law as she had been doing. Plus, she didn't want to—she wanted more flexibility. So she went back to school to get her master's degree in psychology. That way, she figured she could make her own schedule, have her own clients, and see them out of the office in her home.

Each time Michelle sensed she was ready for a change, she made it. The Status Quo way would have been to simply suck it up, stick with it, and finish what she set out to do. But Michelle knows better than anyone that trying something and moving on from it doesn't make you a failure. You're just keeping all your options on the table and living out your own adventure.

Don't Dwell on Yesterday, Double Down on Tomorrow

To gain the confidence to take the big risks at the right time, you need to get comfortable with a degree of failure. You need to see for yourself, as we did, that you can bounce back from anything—and emerge smarter, savvier, and tougher than ever!

Yesterday's blown deadline, yesterday's unconvincing pitch, yesterday's bad interview, yesterday's fight with your mom—you gotta leave all that *in* yesterday. That's the past. Today, you're moving on and you're moving up. Boss Ladies don't dwell on what happened, they learn from it and go back to focus on what they're going to *make happen*.

When Antoinette was producing for TV, she failed every other week! In that world, it's just the nature of the beast: you spend a hundred hours on a show, think you've vetted every guest, asked every question, given the host what they need to know, timed everything out—and there are still screwups and mistakes. There's no such thing as hitting pause and filming another take; the show is taping in front of a live studio audience! And if you're the producer, nine times out of ten when something goes wrong on the show—when a guest doesn't deliver by saying what you need them to say, or things that felt fresh in the script fall flat on the screen—it'll be considered your fault, whether it actually is or not.

It's hard—no doubt. Antoinette used to get real down on herself after a show that didn't go well. You feel like you're only as good as your last show, your last pitch, your last idea. Because there's so much *pressure* on your last show, your last pitch, and your last idea. If it goes well, you feel like ten million dollars! If it goes poorly, you feel like you lost ten million dollars! And it's not just the entertainment business that's like this. In so many jobs, it's easy to feel like you *are* a reflection of your work, to think that a single failure, no matter how small or insignificant, means that *you* are a failure. But you can't treat every single one of your ideas or your attempts as if it were an actual extension of you. Remember: You are not the problem. You are the solution. What's done is done. The task now is moving on. **Never bring yesterday into today.**

Now, let's be realistic: everyone shuts down after a setback. That's okay. When you don't get a job you wanted or you lose out on an account you thought you'd landed or you flub an audition or bomb your stand-up set, you're gonna feel lousy and blue and hangry—like you're a fraud, a failure, like you're never going to do anything good again. That's normal.

But before you ride that express train all the way downtown to Self-Loathing Junction (with a connection to Let's All Give Up Boulevard), slam on those brakes and get the F off that train! Give your-self a set window of time to shut down and feel all your feelings—and then get them out of your system. Take a walk, call your best friend, eat a cheeseburger (and maybe some ice cream too; hey, we don't judge). When Antoinette walked off the set after a bad show, she would always make plans to hang out with people she loved, like her crew or Tricia or a boyfriend—people she didn't have to impress or deliver anything to. Do what you need to do. But get it done—and get it over with.

Once you have a good cathartic cry, you need to shift your focus from Yesterday to Today and on to Tomorrow. You need to ask your-self, *What went wrong? What have I learned?* and then *What can I do differently next time?*

Don't let the Status Quo get inside your head with all that fear, indecision, and second-guessing. If you're second-guessing yourself, the Status Quo wins. If you're paralyzed by indecision, the Status Quo wins. If you're fearing fear, the Status Quo wins. Here's how *you* win: **embrace your fear, along with your own audacity.** They're the same thing, really, in the end, because the Status Quo wants you to fear your own power, your own audacity. Instead, you need to double down on them.

Listen, there are always going to be things in life you can't control—but you get to decide what you want to achieve and how you want to do it. You get to decide if you're going to be a person who goes along to get along or a person who looks fear straight in the eye and goes for it. You get to decide if you're going to let setbacks define you or merely refine you. You get to decide if you've got the power over yourself or if you will cede that power to the Status Quo.

If you want to make an impact, you have to get off the straight and narrow path, put down the instruction manual, get out of your safe zone. Take a risk. Do something differently. Find your White

Space. If you're not trying to do something new, something original, something that hasn't been done before, what's the point? And when you're trying to make a difference, you're gonna have to take some leaps of faith. No one got anywhere just standing around, waiting for something to happen. **Don't let the Status Quo hijack your confidence, or your soul.**

On the Download

When the going gets tough, you just need to get tougher.
Don't let the Status Quo lure you away from your intentions.

The only way to truly fail is by failing to try.
The Status Quo likes to scare us into never trying anything new, or changing the way things are, or going after what's better. But no one got anywhere just standing around, waiting for something to happen.

Go big or go home.
If you're playing to win, you have to be willing to lose. The more audacious the risk, the bigger the reward.

Fear is power waiting to be channeled into success.
Even the toughest Boss Ladies fear failure—whether it's falling short of our own expectations or forgetting to complete that report that's due on the boss's desk. But fear is a powerful motivator. When the pressure is on, start to see that fear can be an opportunity to perform at your best.

At a Decisive Moment, go all-in.
When the dust finally settles, the light shines through, and you see what's what, seize the opportunity in front of you and make a break for it.

Never bring yesterday into today.
What's happened has happened. Now you need to focus on what's ahead. You are defined by who you are, all the time, not how you did on one presentation, one pitch, or one project. So allow yourself a quick pity party, then move on.

Embrace your fear, along with your own audacity.
Fear is uncomfortable, but that's because it's bubbling energy that you need to refine into jet fuel to power your ascent to the stars. The flip side of fear is audacity—the confidence to go out and get yours.

Don't let the Status Quo hijack your confidence, or your soul.

As you're playing the Long Game, there'll be times that the Status Quo will make you question yourself and your decisions. Don't give in to the Status Quo sabotage! Stay true to yourself and stay the course.

A Boss Lady doesn't follow fashions, she leads them.

Be true to yourself by allowing your passions to lead you. You're your best self when you're not trying to be anybody else.

part two

DOUBLE DOWN ON YOUR CREW

chapter five

Don't Network, Connect

We grew up in the Matriarchy. Nothing but strong-willed women for days! There was Grandma at the top, presiding like a benevolent Caribbean Queen: she kept it real and kept us laughing. She may not have graduated high school, but to us she was smarter than Stephen Hawking and a better storyteller than Stephen King. Just walking around the neighborhood with her was an adventure all its own. She spun stories out of the air like it was her job. It wasn't her job, though, it was her passion.

Grandma was born in 1925 in a tiny town in Jamaica—so small it didn't even get its own dot on the map—and raised up four sons and four badass and independent daughters, in whom she instilled a fierce and lasting reverence for education. Her mantra was "No one can take away your education" and she repeated it as often as a nun says Hail Marys. Mom's generation of Bryans left the island in search of good wages, new vistas, and as many degrees as they could earn.

Our generation became the beneficiaries of their wit, wisdom, and worldliness. Eventually, Grandma joined us all in the States, moving a few blocks from where we lived to an apartment building on Turner Place, where she helped raise us up.

It was some Matriarchy, boy, we'll tell you! Those ladies ruled with iron fists—and manicured nails—over the two of us and our cousins: Tracey, Ian, and Michelle. These ladies were badass, plain and simple. Of course, when we were little, we just thought this was how everyone grew up: lots of ladies—kicking ass, taking names—constantly wondering aloud why we hadn't become lawyers or doctors yet (answer: because we were only ten).

Looking back, we see that one of the most valuable lessons Grandma, the Aunts, and Mom taught us was about connection. They all had one another's backs and became better people for it. They also each had their own fiefdoms of knowledge and their own styles for imparting it. And you better believe they imparted it whenever possible. Lucky for us, we were a willing and captive audience!

Aunt Norma was the **Rule Giver**. She was the eldest, so it was her business to know best. She had to set an example, so she followed the rules and made damn sure they were followed by others. From her, we learned how to behave in front of "company," how to carry ourselves, how to comport. Aunt Norma had gone to nursing school in Scotland before we were born, and it seemed like she picked up some Old World etiquette from those rugged hills. Having lunch with her was like having lunch with the Queen of England—or at least Mary, Queen of Scots. She taught us where the napkin goes, where the glass sits, and which fork is for which course. She didn't mess around.

NETTE
Can you pass the lemonade?

> **AUNT NORMA**
> Can you pass the lemonade, *please*.

> **TRISH**
> I think we're gonna go outside now.

> **AUNT NORMA**
> You mean you're *going* outside? Are you *thinking* about it, or are you actually *doing* it?

If we made a mistake, Aunt Norma let us know. She was so intense, sometimes we got tired even *thinking* about going to visit her. We knew she was gonna be correcting us all the time!

Thing was: we sorta liked it. Aunt Norma knew *what* was *what*. And not just what she picked up from Scotland and the UK. Aunt Norma had traveled halfway across the world in the other direction, too. She took a dim view of our shenanigans and lackadaisical American manners generally; she wanted to make sure we grew up to be cultured and polite. Except for our frequent use of the word *gonna*, we're gonna go ahead and say: Mission Accomplished!

Aunt Leonie was the **Caretaker**. She knew what people needed even before *they* knew they needed it! Aunt Leonie was the master of her castle, and her castle was the kitchen. Watching her cook was like watching Billie Holiday sing: it was her art. All the Aunts, and obviously Grandma, knew how to whip up killer Jamaican food—oxtail, stew peas, curry shrimp, roti, or stew chicken—but Aunt Leonie was the only one who fully embraced American cooking. She could make *anything*. We loved to eat stuff we saw the TV sitcom kids eating, and so did our cousin Michelle, Aunt Leonie's daughter.

Whenever we went to their apartment, we used to rush to the

pantry and fridge with the gusto we now reserve only for a Barneys sample sale.

> **TRISH**
> Damn, what *is* half this stuff?

> **NETTE**
> Not sure. Let's eat it!

There were gourmet snacks, dried fruit the likes of which we had never seen, premade dishes like lasagna and turkey chili (from the fancy grocery store Citarella), and individually wrapped cookies that looked too good to eat (until we ate them). And then for dinner, she made hamburgers *and* french fries! Or pasta primavera, served with fresh garlic bread and a quarter wheel of fresh Parmesan cheese that we could grate to our cheesy hearts' delight.

So obviously we worshipped Aunt Leonie, but it wasn't just about the food. She was the queen of gift giving and knew where to find *everything*—like the rare Cabbage Patch Kids that were the envy of our classmates, back when that was our jam. The other Aunts didn't like to admit it, but they all used to ask Aunt Leonie to pick out a gift for the others, or for us, because she had such a sixth sense about it. She was the only aunt—actually, make that the only person in our lives—who bought us separate and distinct gifts on our birthday and Christmas. One year, she got Tricia a new pair of Nikes and Antoinette a doll that had changing outfits and a set of makeup. Aunt Leonie taught us how to *see* other people—and how to let them know it.

Aunt Monica, well, she was the **Boss Lady**—and she was a Boss Lady before anyone thought to put those two words together. Damn, she was *empowered.* She ran her own construction company that specialized in window installations. But not just your run-of-the-mill window installations. Aunt Monica's company did the windows for the prestigious Stuyvesant High School down in Lower Manhattan, one of the big midtown Chase Bank buildings, and the iconic Guastavino's Restaurant on the Upper East Side. She had to keep a lot of men who worked under her in line—and looking back, we're pretty sure she also had to deal with some tough characters. We saw her work once, onsite, in her element, and we were not at all surprised to observe that she didn't take shit from anyone. She walked around, pointing *here* and *there*, scoffing at unrolled blueprints, and swearing like a sailor when she needed to get a point across (sometimes in Jamaican slang, but only when she *really, really* needed to get her point across).

And, besides all that, as you might remember, she could braid hair like nobody's business. Aunt Monica was legit.

Aunt Monica was the only aunt to move out of Brooklyn. But not because she wanted to run away; she was living the American Dream, and she wanted all of us to visit whenever we could. We spent every major holiday out there in the suburbs of Long Island because her house was the only place where the whole family could fit. We're talking snow in the backyard and a big Douglas fir tree in the living room, sparkling with multicolor lights and shiny ornaments. It was magical. We still remember the year she bought these majestic angel figurines that she liked to put near the tippy-top of the tree, where they still circle every December to this day!

Aunt Monica worked hard, and she played hard. She made bank and she reinvested it in her family, making sure that our cousins Tracey and Ian were well taken care of. But she also made sure they did all their homework, and if they didn't, you better believe they were bound to get cursed out, like they were one of Aunt Monica's lazy foremen caught napping on the job.

Then there was Mom, who you already know was the **Swiss Army Knife**. She was the youngest, a single mom, and she hustled harder than anyone else we've ever met. Yet somehow she made it look easy.

Last, but definitely not least, there was Grandma. She was the **Heart and Soul**. She didn't have all that many opportunities handed to her growing up, so she created them for herself and those around her. She worked well into her sixties (which was like seventies in today's years) to help make our lives possible. She wanted her grandchildren to feel as well off as any of the other kids. She hooked it up. If she wasn't reading books or newspapers in her special chair— literally the only thing she ever owned that she didn't like to share— then she was taking us on one of her adventures: maybe a stroll down the block to a new park, or farther afield to a new neighborhood. Grandma wanted to create a feeling of belonging at all times. For her, culture was ritual. She practiced it all the time, and she made sure to instill it in us, too. It got to the point that even our mom tried to pump the brakes on some of her Jamaican-ness. Like when Grandma used to sing us this classic nursery rhyme:

> *Mama gone to market,*
> *Papa gone to Kingston,*
> *Buy candy for baby,*
> *Baby eats it all,*
> *Gives Nancy none,*
> *Nancy pick up baby,*
> *Throw her on the ground.*
> *Clap on, clap on,*
> *Wait till Mama come home.*

We're still not sure what the moral of that one is—and maybe Mom isn't either. But it delighted Grandma, and therefore us—we would squeal every time she got to the "Clap on, clap on" part.

Just as Mom was the runt of the litter in her generation, we were the youngest in ours. There were Aunt Monica's kids, Tracey and Ian, eight and ten years older than us, and Aunt Leonie's daughter, Michelle, who was only six years older but who seemed, for most of our childhood, like a full-on grown-up. So we learned a ton from them, too.

From Tracey, we got our aspiration for cool. We thought her life was *amazing*. Not only did she live in a real house, with a backyard, but she had about a hundred trophies: from track and field *and* basketball! We decided that she could have easily been a cast member of *Beverly Hills 90210,* and whenever she wasn't around we figured she was kicking it with Brenda and Kelly at the Peach Pit.*

From Michelle, we saw the value of hard work and studying. She was so focused on her academics, she hardly had time for us. That is, unless we helped quiz her for a math or history test using her meticulously detailed notecards. We held them up like Vanna White and she aced them like Venus Williams. She was more likely to be hanging out at the library than the Peach Pit, but she showed us that smart was cool, too. And then, to round it out, we had each other. And we're awesome!

The point is that growing up, we did not lack for real, meaningful connections with people we looked up to. For all that we learned from our family, the most important lesson we took away was that all the best moments in life are shared. When we look back on our lives thus far, we see that all our happiest moments, the times we were the most elated, the proudest, the most joyous, were when we were in the company of other people: friends, or family, and mostly each other! Having a tribe to share your ups and downs with is one of the

---

* And Ian helped offset all the feminine energy. He was one cool guy. He didn't need to say much but when he did it was dosed with wit and sarcasm.

greatest joys in life. That's not to say it isn't also very hard work. Your people can be up in your shit! Like the time that the Aunts vetoed our junior year of high school spring break trip to Cancún even after Mom said yes.

> **AUNTS**
> You're not going unsupervised with boys and alcohol.

> **TRISH AND NETTE**
> We already bought tickets.

> **AUNTS**
> Guess those tickets will fly by themselves.

Sometimes your people test you and your patience. But there's nothing more valuable in life than a deep connection. That's why we go into all our relationships with an open heart and mind. It's why we seek out gurus, why we're hungry to surround ourselves with people who might know more than we do. And it's why we always share what we have learned with others and become gurus to those who are looking to move up.

In the first part of *Double Down* we focused on all the skills, tools, and tactics to help you become your best self—confident, cool, compassionate, courageous—on your journey to the top. We hope that we've helped you identify your superpowers, be on the lookout for White Space, focus on the Long Game to reach your North Star, roll with the punches, and be willing to take risks, face your fears, and defy the Status Quo along the way.

But if our tribe of Matriarchs taught us anything, it's that no woman is an island. To be your best self, it isn't enough to double down just on yourself; you also have to double down on those people in your life who you can bet on, and who will bet on you, too.

This chapter is about how to cultivate the kinds of relationships that matter—and then double down on them. We'll teach you the principles of forming strong connections, and we'll focus on how to connect with gurus, people like our aunts, who can become guides for you on your journey to the top. In all your relationships, we'll counsel you to discard Bullshit Status Quo definitions of connections in favor of true connections that benefit you both.

Curiosity Breeds Connection

Everyone knows connections are everything, right? Connections are introductions, connections are informational interviews (that lead to real interviews), connections are referrals, connections are mentorships, connections are friends, connections are opportunities. If you know the right people, you can get into the dope party where you might meet your idol or a new business partner. If you know the right people, you'll get discovered and become famous. If you know the right people, your work will be seen and you'll be recognized for who you've always known yourself to be.

Maybe so. Yes. Sometimes.

Connections may help you get your foot in the door. But real relationships—true connections—will help you blast the door off its hinges.

The Status Quo wants you to be jaded about connections. It wants you to think connections are only what rich kids have: Daddy went to Harvard and donates money, so his son will get preferential treatment. Mommy sits on a board with the CEO of a company, so her daughter gets the coveted internship out of college. The Status Quo wants you to think that connections are something either you're born with or you're not.

Yes, some people are blessed with these sorts of connections—

and maybe you aren't one of them. Them's the breaks. But what the Status Quo doesn't want you to realize is that those kinds of connections have the shelf life of a Snapchat selfie; they're nice in the short term, but they don't stick around for long. That's because they revolve around what you *get out of them*—that acceptance letter, that invite, that internship—rather than what you bring to and bring away from them. If you think about connections only in a transactional way, as a means to an end, you'll never get anything meaningful out of your relationships with anyone.

It's the get-rich-quick theory of networking. And it's fine with the Status Quo.

The Status Quo *wants* you to think you're moving on up in the world when in reality you're just making shallow and convenient alliances with people who only seem important. It wants you to think that once you get that invite, that reference, that referral, it's game over: the big corner office is yours, and you're ready to expense a $200 lunch on the company card! The Status Quo wants you to make the biggest mistake of all: thinking that *who* you know is more important than *what* you know. Alliances aren't real relationships. And "networking" probably *won't* lead to exciting new opportunities so much as it will lead to unexciting new Instagram followers.

Know this: the place where it all starts is with learning. If you're not learning from the people around you, you're not moving forward. And if you're not moving forward, you might as well pack your bags, lace up your sneakers, and head home.

And also know this: at the heart of learning—and therefore every good relationship—is a mutual curiosity. That may sound strange. But think about it. Have you ever respected a leader you were *not* curious about, who you *didn't* think could teach you something? Have you ever sought out someone and built a rapport with them and *not* thought that they possessed some cool quality that piqued your interest?

By the same token, do you think any leader has taken an interest in your professional development who *didn't* think she could benefit in some way from the relationship? Do you think that anyone who's ever sought you out or asked you to lunch *didn't* find you interesting in some way? Whether with peers or gurus, both parties need to be curious about the other for the connections to be real, to be authentic, to be fruitful. No matter what stage you're at in your career, it pays to cultivate those kinds of relationships—to know not just how to seek them out but also how to see them through.

From the time we were kids being raised in the Matriarchy, to girls strolling through our neighborhood (barbershop, Marlborough stoop, park), to young women book-learning at Catholic high school and a liberal arts college, we've understood the importance of cultivating the ability to connect. And in the workplace we've witnessed lots of different tactics deployed, we've tried many ourselves, and we've concluded that none are nearly as powerful, or as rewarding, as the connections that flow from curiosity.

In fact, when we think about all our best relationships over the years, three related principles have held true, whether we were meeting impressive people at events, finding new work buddies, securing the help of a guru, or just making new friends. These principles are surprisingly simple, but crucial to keep in mind as you navigate your world.

Three Principles of Connection

1. BE WHO YOU ARE, NOT WHO YOU THINK YOU SHOULD BE

It might seem obvious, but you can't be your best self if you're always trying to be someone else! Most people never totally figure out who they are; they're not brave enough to look within and do the work. People really connect only with those who are confident, cool, and compassionate—remember the Three Cs—and people who know who they are broadcast those qualities the quickest. That's why we always try to lean into our authentic strengths and our authentic interests—we don't front—because most people can spot a faker quicker than they can swipe left. Remember you can't be everyone else! You can't even be *anyone* else! You're stuck being *you*—and that's a good thing! Be curious about other people; don't try to *be* other people.

2. MATCH PASSIONS, NOT PROFESSIONS

Whether you're meeting people at a party, trying to up your game at a conference or event, or seeking out the guidance of someone with more experience than you, you should always find emotional touch-points to establish or deepen your connection. By this we don't mean shit like "Oh, you work in television? I work in television too!" or "You work for a nontraditional start-up that focuses on creating story-led experiences for brands? So do I!" How many times have you seen people's eyes glaze over while you told them about what you do? And how many times have you stood there, listening dutifully, with one eye trained on the hors d'oeuvres while they told you what *they* do? Boy, we got bored even thinking about it! You've played out this scene too many times to count, we're guessing, and yet how many of those people actually made a true and lasting impression?

We all have a default script we launch into when someone asks us what we do. But who says we have to follow it? As passionate as we are about our jobs, we know that isn't an excuse to talk people's ears off about it. When people are following a script, they're not entirely themselves, they're playing a role, they're on autopilot. They want to seem in control—and if they're focused on being in control, they won't be able to open up to you. Looking back, we see that all our most genuine and professionally beneficial relationships grew out of times we connected with people over nonwork topics—music, TV, food, travel. So get curious about who other people *are*, not what they *do*.

3. LEAD WITH WHAT YOU'VE GOT, NOT WHAT YOU NEED

You know when you can just *feel* that someone *wants* something from you? Your mom calls you up on a Sunday, and even before you pick up you know she's gonna casually ask when you're coming over to help her set up her Roku. Or your boyfriend comes into the living room and uses that syrupy voice he thinks is sweet, but you can tell he's about to hit you up for a favor. Or your male coworker whom you rarely speak to stops you in the hallway and asks how your weekend was, and you just know that he's trying to butter you up before asking you to look over some work he's done—by which he of course means complete it for him. Yeah, so you know *that* feeling? That's what it feels like to be in the presence of a Taker—and exactly *zero* good connections are made that way. So don't be a Taker, be a Maker. Get curious about what other people need—then find a way to help them get it.

Don't Seek Out Mentors, Get Gurus

When we talk about gurus, it isn't just another way of saying "mentor." The reasons for having one might be the same—to get someone successful and established to double down on you—but there's a key difference. Mentor and sponsor relationships tend to be more of a means to an end; we seek them out for a specific need or purpose, like to show us the ropes at a new job, to help us break into a new industry, or to grant us access to a network. A guru, on the other hand, is a guide. Mentors widen our network, or help us up the corporate ladder; gurus widen our horizons and help us toward our North Star.

There are three classic mistakes people make when it comes to gurus: (1) thinking you don't need one, (2) seeking out ones only on the basis of their job title, and (3) forgetting to make clear what *you* offer *them*. Any one of these mistakes can cost you—and cost you big.

Our culture celebrates the narrative of the lone genius and lavishes praise on people who seem "self-sufficient"—people who act like they don't need help from anyone. This is a classic Status Quo myth that can be crippling if you buy into it. When you hear about super successful people, it's easy to forget they were once young and inexperienced just like everyone else—driven but in need of direction, passionate but not yet polished, hungry without any table manners. But the truth is that anyone who gets anywhere in life has had help from someone, probably *many* someones, who instilled confidence, provided valuable feedback, and allowed room for growth. And everyone who has risen up the ranks of any profession knows exactly who the people are who helped them along the way—especially when they were starting out.

These are the people we call gurus—people we position ourselves to learn from. Much like our OG gurus, the Matriarchs, these are the folks who believed in you even before *you* believed in you. Whether it's a teacher, boss, peer, or family member, it is an incalculable advantage to have an ally in your corner who knows more than you do and who is willing to share the lessons they've already learned, usually the hard way, so that you don't have to.

The Status Quo will try to tell you to pick a guru on the basis of status—no surprise there!—and that's a trap that's all too easy to fall into. When you're starting out in your career, or transitioning into a new job, or learning the ropes of a new industry, it's tempting to try to ingratiate yourself with the person who has the most power or the fanciest office. This is a huge mistake. Just because a person has power or a fancy title doesn't mean they have something to teach you. Don't think that just because you cozy up to a high-level person they'll shower you with favors to help you get ahead. If you wanna know the truth, you're actually better off staying away from the people who already *have* a lot of power, or a lot of acolytes sucking up to them all the time, as they're likely more into *feeling* like a guru than actually *being* one. You should seek out people you respect and admire, regardless of where they sit on the company org chart. Don't just fall in line behind the others vying to get noticed by that same person at the top. Remember: if there's one thing Boss Ladies don't do, it's wait in line.

Last thing: gurus already know *they* possess knowledge or experience that is valuable, so you better make it clear—and quick—why they should invest their time and energy in *you*. They aren't going to just show up one day and offer to hold your hand, give you a pep talk, or stay late at the office teaching you a new skill—they have shit to do, checks to write, hands to shake! It's up to you to seek them out, prove yourself, and convince them their investment in you will be worthwhile.

If you're thinking, *But I don't have anything of value to offer*, think again. Keep in mind that even if people know more than you do about whatever area or field they're an expert in, that doesn't mean they know *everything*. In fact, people who are highly knowledgeable or experienced in one field—people who have focused on that one area so intently and for so long—tend to know much less about adjacent ones. And in that lies a golden opportunity for you to uphold *your* end of the value exchange by helping them fill in those gaps. Trust us: we've proved ourselves to many a guru over the years simply by sharing our insights and knowledge about technology, pop culture, and fashion. Deb Esayian was one of them.

When Tricia met Deb for the first time, she wasn't actively seeking out a guru. She wasn't really even trying to impress or attract attention. Tricia and Deb just happened to cross paths, so they struck up a conversation.

This was back during Tricia's first stint at Emmis, when she was working in sales, trying to convince clients to advertise on one of Emmis's radio stations. Deb had recently transferred to the New York office and was working for corporate, trying to develop a job board—like Monster or CareerBuilder, which were big at the time—that would leverage Emmis's command of their radio audience, advertising job listings for multicultural applicants on the airwaves.

One morning, Deb and Tricia ran into each other walking into the office, down on Hudson and Houston in the old Carpenters Union Building. At this point, they knew each other by sight, but they'd never spoken. They had no overlap in their jobs; Deb worked in a totally different business area. Deb was way senior to Tricia, but because Tricia didn't work for her, it didn't occur to her to be intimidated. So they just got to talking—you know, the way you do. Deb mentioned her interest in horses and horse racing, and Tricia told her she'd gone to Skidmore, so she'd lived just a few minutes away from the big horse-racing tracks in Saratoga Springs.

Deb was short—but she had a commanding presence. When she spoke, people listened. It was quickly clear to Tricia that Deb knew her shit. She was like a miniencyclopedia, particularly when it came to topics like culture, museums, and history. Tricia found her totally fascinating.

Once the ice had been broken, they established a kind of rapport and would chat whenever they ran into each other, whether it was over by the office photocopier, in the elevator, or in the beautiful, high-ceilinged old lobby of the building. Tricia had never met someone who was so into horses and racing, and she was dying to learn more. Tricia told Deb about her side hustle—at the time we were promoting parties in the East Village for extra cash—and Deb was intrigued. They were so different, but they shared the same kind of curiosity.

Eventually, they got to the point where they would just banter back and forth, like characters in a sitcom.

>   **DEB**
> So, do you have any pets?

>   **TRICIA**
> Pets? Please. If I was gonna get a pet,
> I might as well get a kid.

>   **DEB**
> But do you like dogs?

>   **TRICIA**
> I like dogs I know.

>   **DEB**
> What does that even mean—*I like dogs I know*?

> ### TRICIA
> Like if my friend has a dog and he's cute,
> I like him. But I don't have a special need
> to pet dogs I don't know on the street.
> Wait—are you a street-dog-petter?
>
> ### DEB
> Yes! I love dogs.

These interactions weren't particularly sophisticated, and they had nothing to do with work. They were just real, authentic exchanges with no agenda, two people shooting the shit and being themselves. Neither of them had expectations of the other—beyond the expectation that they'd have a good conversation every time they were together.

But over the next twelve months was when Tricia began to get fed up with the lack of opportunity for growth at Emmis—*Wait your turn, pay your dues*—and she had a meeting with the GM of Emmis, Judy Ellis, where she was quite literally told to *pay her dues* and *wait her turn*. Tricia said no thanks, and off she went, guns blazing, into the Wild West of the first dot-com boom. Then, after she'd been working at Excite for about six months, she got a call from an unknown number.

It was Deb.

Deb asked Tricia if she would meet for lunch. Remembering Tricia's fondness for nice restaurants, she quickly added, "Don't worry, I'll take you out to a fancy lunch!"

Deb didn't have to twist Tricia's arm. And true to her word, a week later, they met at the Grand Central Oyster Bar. If you've never been, it's the kind of place that always makes you feel important—the elegant marble pillars, the history, the fresh oysters, the crazed commuters rushing to catch their trains . . . It's classic.

They spent the first thirty minutes chatting, shooting the shit just like old times. Then Deb got down to it.

DEB

Now, let's get down to it. You're probably wondering why I asked you here today.

In truth, Tricia had assumed that Deb just wanted to catch up. But as she quickly figured out, that wasn't all. Deb explained that Emmis had tasked her with launching a digital division to give the radio stations an online presence and create more opportunities to sell ads, while courting a new audience. Deb wanted Tricia to come back to help lead the project, which would be company-wide.

DEB

You know digital. You're driven and savvy. It's time you came back and built something new and lasting. What do you say?

Tricia asked if she could sleep on it. She liked Deb, and she liked the idea of moving into a new White Space, but as she thought about it that night and over the next week, those old Status Quo doubts crept into her head. *Do I know enough about this stuff to really be effective? Am I ready to do this?*

Then she realized: *Deb* thought she could do this, and Deb was no fool. She was a Boss Lady, and what's more, she wasn't just some random Boss Lady. She knew Tricia; they had a genuine connection—if she thought Tricia could pull this off, maybe she could! And that was the dealmaker: if Deb believed in Tricia, and Deb was smart as shit, then, via the transitive property of being smart as shit, Tricia should believe in Tricia!

> TRICIA
>
> Okay, let's do this!

So now Tricia was back at Emmis, but this time to help launch a huge new wing of the company. Deb had doubled down on Tricia, and now Tricia was hell-bent on proving to Deb that she'd made the right bet. The first big task was, well, figuring out *what* the business was and how the hell it would work. There was no blueprint to follow; radio stations didn't know how to approach the Internet yet. So Tricia got on the phone and focus-grouped everyone she knew—friends, friends of friends, old friends, old friends of friends, new friends, new friends of new friends, and old friends of new friends. Basically, everyone ever. And a few weeks later, Tricia came back with a plan that was ten times better and more comprehensive than even Deb was expecting from her.

And thus began an extremely productive partnership. Deb expected a lot from Tricia, and Tricia wanted to live up to those expectations. Tricia got to study Deb's way of working a room and her way with words, packed with figures of speech and metaphors (*neck and neck, not till we cross the finish line, down to the wire, jockeying for position,* and *don't back the wrong horse*). It didn't matter who Deb was meeting with—CEOs, venture capitalists, clients—she knew her audience and could speak to anyone. Everyone respected Deb and wanted her opinion. Tricia would walk out of every meeting thinking, *I want to command a room like that.*

Over the course of their eight-year working relationship, Deb taught Tricia many more lessons than she can count, but two in particular stick out.

(1) **Always make sure you can pay yourself out.**

What she meant was that no one can question your contribution if you're delivering the numbers. A balance sheet don't lie.

(2) In the workplace, perception is reality.

What she meant was: keep your cool. When evangelizing for her ideas, Tricia tended to get caught up in the heat of the moment; she became hotheaded and worked against herself. Deb's advice was to take the emotion out of it and come from a place of facts. When you raise your voice, you lower yourself.

But while Tricia was learning all this and more from Deb, she always made it her job to up Deb's game, too. Tricia might not have been able to work a room quite like Deb—yet!—but remember, she knew digital, and she knew cool. So when it was imperative to increase traffic to the home page, Tricia introduced Deb to the idea of gamification and showed her how it could be used to lure in more users and increase page views. Another time, Tricia explained how they could use their big radio personalities, like Angie Martinez or Funkmaster Flex, to increase their sense of community on the web by creating personality quizzes, host-trivia giveaways, and other games that would keep people engaged on the page.

And that's how it worked: Tricia had the backing of a guru who treated her like an equal and empowered her to do the highest-quality work. And Deb got to draw on the digital and cultural savvy of a passionate and creative up-and-comer whose high-quality work made Deb, herself, look good. They respected each other, learned from each other, and raised each other up. We're guessing you have someone in your life who can do the same for you. So remember: **relationships are two-way streets.** You and your guru strengthen and reinforce each other, in your own ways. You need them, and you need to make them need you.

There's No Such Thing as Too Many Gurus

It really all comes back to that one key principle: curiosity breeds connection. If you're open and receptive to learning from people, rather than just hell-bent on showing them how much you know or angling to extract something from them, you can connect with almost anyone.

Antoinette is a master at finding and holding down gurus wherever she goes. At *The Tyra Banks Show* alone Antoinette had three! And you can bet she took advantage of the opportunity to learn from their different styles.

John Redmann was the **Host Whisperer**. John had worked with so many daytime TV icons, like Wayne Brady and Rosie O'Donnell, that he'd developed an incredible ability to deal with talent—to boost their confidence, to reassure them that a minor issue wasn't a major problem, and to assuage their anxiety when something real went wrong. He had a way with words—both choosing them wisely and delivering them well. He was always direct, but soft. From him, Antoinette learned: (3) **tell people the truth just as if you were telling them what they want to hear.**

Alex Duda was the **Elevator**. On Friday afternoons, when everyone was staring at their computer monitor daydreaming about the weekend, Tyra would give Alex her notes for the next week's show—most of which raised questions about this or that idea. And by raised questions, we mean: she vetoed things. As in: *I don't like this segment. This feels thin. What else do we have?* It was Alex's job to turn this feedback into action—no easy feat when all the producers felt like their souls had just been crushed by a trash compactor!

Even though her notes invariably involved more work for Antoinette and her fellow producers, Alex was able to direct dejection into forward momentum. She taught Antoinette: **(4) if you give people a path forward and a nudge, they will blaze the trail.** Alex gave people hope and enthusiasm, which is the most powerful motivator there is!

Rachel Miskowiec was the **Hype Queen**, because she could take any idea to the Next Level. She knew how to produce greatness within a budget. She was a master at finding that one layer, that one detail, that one line to make a segment fire. When Antoinette was planning a show on makeovers on the streets in Manhattan, for example, Rachel suggested they instead get a double decker bus, drive around the city, and do a makeover in every borough. She showed Antoinette: **(5) there's *always* one more detail you can improve.**

And back at *The Montel Williams Show,* there was Diane, who gave Antoinette her first job in television. Diane was the producer who stopped Antoinette when she was leaving that informational interview and complimented her on her dope AF outfit! Cool, confident, and unflappable, Diane was the **Rock**. Nothing, it seemed, could shake her; she took every challenge in stride. Prior to joining Montel, she'd worked at *The Oprah Winfrey Show* as an attorney but got talked into transitioning into producing because her ideas were so good!

When Antoinette started at Montel, she didn't know what to expect. The culture was very different from that of her last job, working in communications for the mayor's office. She quickly learned that in talk shows there are no rules. You need to chase stories like a bloodhound, and you're often competing against your colleagues to have your story told. It was fast-paced and could get catty and intense. Toward the end of her first week, Antoinette was already having second thoughts: *What did I get myself into?*

Then Antoinette thought about Diane.

Diane was calm and collected, with a quiet yet commanding

presence—she spoke only when she needed to, and then everyone listened, rapt. Diane was always in control, even though there were plenty of reasons for her to lose it—when another show beat them to a story they'd been laboring on, when a show went *crazy* over-budget and rated poorly, when a producer quit without giving two weeks' notice and left the rest of the team to pick up the slack. Diane's attitude was: *What good is freaking out when so many people are counting on me?* If Diane could keep it together in this chaotic environment, Antoinette thought, then maybe she could, too.

One night, Antoinette was working late on a story when Diane stopped by her desk on her way out of the office. Antoinette told Diane what she was working on and about the person she was trying to track down, and Diane listened, nodded, and said, "That sounds very promising. Just remember: Always get the other side. You always want to get the other side, the other perspective; that's how you get the most interesting interaction. And it's how you get the truth."

Antoinette thanked her for the advice and asked about the unopened bottle of wine in Diane's hand. It turned out Diane was a wine aficionado, and the bottle she had in her hand was a Pinot Noir, en route to her wine cellar. Antoinette had recently gotten into the whole wine thing herself, and they immediately bonded. A week or two later, during another late night, Diane stopped with a different bottle and asked if Antoinette wanted to try it with her. That was an offer she couldn't refuse!

Meanwhile, during the workday, Antoinette studied how Diane rolled. She expected a lot of everyone, but she never micromanaged— she didn't need to. From Day One, she instilled the sense that results spoke louder than words. She told Antoinette, "If you think you have a good idea for a show, go for it—go for it *hard*."

Soon after, in the run-up to February sweeps, Antoinette was chasing a story that everyone wanted. It involved a guy who was now in jail for a string of highly publicized crimes, and everyone was pulling out all the stops trying to get his parents, and the parents of his victims, to talk. All the daytime shows wanted the exclusive—and all the prime-time ones did too. Antoinette had been calling the boy's parents on speed dial for days and wasn't getting anywhere, but she refused to give up. Finally, she got the mother on the phone. Antoinette opened up about her own life and suggested that going on *The Montel Williams Show* could be good for the family: when you get people to talk about things, maybe even see them from the other side, she pointed out, everyone is more capable of moving on and growing after hardship. The mother seemed unconvinced, but a few weeks later, right in the middle of sweeps, she changed her tune. She was in! Antoinette was ecstatic. She worked up an outline for the segment and brought it to Diane.

> DIANE
> This is terrific. You should pitch Montel
> directly.

> ANTOINETTE
> Seriously?

> DIANE
> Yes, this is your show. Your title doesn't
> matter. This is good, and I think he'll see
> it. Just make it good. And, if you do,
> I think this could be the full hour.

To Antoinette's ears, that was like hearing she'd won the lottery! The Full Hour of the show dedicated to the idea she'd been working so hard on? That was the holy grail of daytime! She was nervous about pitching to Montel himself, of course, but she could tell that Diane believed in her, and that gave her the confidence to believe in herself. So despite her apprehension, she pitched it, and, well, you can probably guess where this story is going.

Not only did she get the Full Hour, but when the show finally aired, it ended up being one of the highest-rated shows of the year!

Antoinette learned many valuable lessons from Diane (not least being the difference between a Pinot Noir and a Côtes du Rhône), but the one that really stuck was this: **(6) fear helps no one.** Diane taught her to be relentless in her pursuit of a story and fearless in advocating for herself and her ideas. And most important, Diane showed her the power of having someone in your corner who takes a chance on you, sees the potential in you, and doubles down on it.

Once Antoinette was promoted to producer and assumed an even bigger role in coming up with story ideas and influencing the feel of the show, she continued to heed the advice Diane had given her early on: "If you think you have a good idea for a show, go for it—go for it *hard*." At one point, Antoinette came to Diane with the idea to push the envelope of the show's format to incorporate *less* drama, more lifestyle. Diane was receptive and asked what Antoinette had in mind. Antoinette had come up with a whole plan, a full hour of the show where celebrities would cohost with Montel, doing stories on pop culture and makeovers but focusing on *the people behind the stories,* rather than simply showcasing some hot new album or some trendy new hairstyle.

Diane liked what she heard, and together they brought the fleshed-out idea to Montel. He'd noticed how much trust Diane had been putting in Antoinette lately, and that made him even more receptive to her idea.

One of the first shows they tried was a makeover—but with a twist. Antoinette found a doctor who specialized in implanting a new kind of hearing aid that was said to work wonders and got him to agree to perform the operation for free in exchange for airtime. Then Antoinette and her team found a woman who had been deaf her whole life and filmed her before and after the surgery, right there in the studio. The operation was a success, and when Montel brought out the woman's son and husband the audience got to experience that incredible moment when she heard their voices for the first time, right then and there! It had been a risky idea from the start, but Antoinette couldn't have been happier that she went for it.

After Antoinette had been at Montel for five years, Diane told her that she was finally leaving for a new show.

> **ANTOINETTE**
> Oh. Well, congrats! That's amazing.

> **DIANE**
> And I'd like to take two producers with me.
> You're one of them. What do you say?

Antoinette said yes, and off they went to their next adventure together!

Diane trusted Antoinette, and over time her faith began to rub off. Above all she learned: (7) **a good guru always recognizes the potential in you before you do.** That's why you need to find the people who will unlock what's already inside you, so that you can harness that power to unlock the potential in others.

Even now that she's reached the point in her career where younger women look at her as a guru, Antoinette maintains and seeks out relationships with gurus of her own. The Status Quo would have you believe that once "you've arrived" you don't need any more help from anyone. The Status Quo also wants you to believe that asking for help makes you seem incompetent or weak. But the truth is that Boss Ladies *respect* other Boss Ladies who seek out help or advice. No matter where we are in our careers, we are all students as much as we are teachers, and the more you always remain open to learning from the wise people around you, the more wisdom you'll have to impart.

On the Download

True relationships are more than a means to an end.
You should never be seeking something tangible out of a possible connection—other than making a strong connection. If you're searching, you'll be lost. If you're hunting, you'll go home empty-handed.

Connection is curiosity.
If you're genuinely interested in other people, they will be genuinely interested in you—unless they're interested only in themselves, in which case, move on! Curiosity is the heart of connection, because the openness and confidence that curiosity needs to exist are irresistible to others.

Three Principles of Connection

1. **Be who you are, not who you think you should be.** You can't be your best self if you're always trying to be someone else.

2. **Match passions, not professions.** We all have a default script we launch into when someone asks us what we do. But who says we have to follow it? Get curious about who other people are, not what they do.

3. **Lead with what you've got, not with what you need.** Real, fruitful relationships are a two-way street. If you're looking to gain insight from a master, you'll need to prove that you're worthy of her wisdom. No matter where you are in your career, you will have valuable pockets of knowledge that you can bring to the table. Share them!

Teachings of the Gurus

- Always make sure you can pay yourself out.

- In the workplace, perception is reality.

- Tell people the truth just as if you were telling them what they wanted to hear.

- If you give people a path forward and a nudge, they will blaze the trail.

- There's always one more thing you can improve.

- Fear helps no one.

- A good guru always recognizes the potential in you before you do.

chapter six

Don't Inherit Your Tribe, Build It

In the apartment building we grew up in, there were Caribbean kids and white kids, middle-class African Americans and middle-class Indians. Down the block, there were Jewish kids on the south side, Hispanics on the north. There were Italians out delivering pizzas, and Irish Catholics fixing the plumbing.

On summer Saturday afternoons, heat radiated from the asphalt, and water ran from the opened hydrant. Kids splashed and giggled and played, like something out of a black-and-white photo from the 1940s. The trees offered pools of shaded refuge from the sun's pounding heat. In those oases, we drank quarter water from the corner bodegas to quench our thirst and feed our need for sugar. The day was full of possibility. And how to spend it was entirely up to us.

We could roll back into our building to see what our neighbors were up to, maybe score a beef patty with some greens or practice our dance moves with our girlfriends (Tricia was perfecting her moonwalk). We could go down the block to see what the Corner Kids were up to, probably eating twenty-five-cent bags of chips and chopping it up about everything from music to the latest Polo gear. We could go chill on the stoop with the dudes, their shiny boombox blasting reggae dance hall or hip-hop—Special Ed, Big Daddy Kane, Shabba, Buju—as they puffed out clouds of cigarette or blunt smoke (which we'd have to avoid like dodgeballs in gym so that Mom didn't catch a whiff).

We could head over to the Brooklyn Public Library on Cortelyou—quite possibly the city's tiniest branch—to spend an hour or two roaming the stacks and basking in the cool breeze of the temperamental A/C. Or we could hit the subway stop, where the neighborhood boys would be sporting herringbone chains and gold caps on their teeth, probably up to no good but making it look fun, holding court on the steps like they owned the place.

In short, the world was at our fingertips.

The neighborhood, Ditmas Park, was where it all happened. It was our playground, our IRL Facebook, our minimall, our commons. Ditmas Park was where we learned the art and science of the mix and the mingle, the hustle and the flow, the give and the get, and the importance of building a crew that was tight, thick, and diverse as hell.

We loved how different everyone was—and how much we all had to learn from one another. No one had a complete view of the world, or even the neighborhood. It was like a jigsaw puzzle: you had to piece together one block, one corner, one conversation at a time. And because we were so used to being open with each other—thanks to our Twinity—we took that attitude with us into all our interactions around the neighborhood, and beyond. We loved talking to pretty much anybody.

Sometimes Mom wished we weren't quite so open!

Take the Lo Life Crew, for example.

The Lo Life Crew were a bunch of hustlers out of Crown Heights and Brownsville who rocked Polo Ralph Lauren gear—hence the Lo—like they were sales clerks running shit at the "Polo Mansion," the flagship on Madison Avenue. Polo was the epitome of preppy white culture, and these boys appropriated, sampled, and remixed that shit, making it their own. They brought Polo into the realm of the cool, where fashion and culture were created on the streets, not curated in a window display. Everyone in the neighborhood knew you were "lo down" if you wore Polo from head to toe.

The Lo Lives had a legit hustle although it wasn't, strictly speaking, a legal one—they boosted Polo T-shirts and pants from Macy's and resold them to everyone we knew. But, hey, they were chasing the American Dream. For our birthdays, we sometimes got cash—and that cash went straight to the Lo Lives because we wanted to rock that country club look, too—whether it was the Rugby collection or the Polo Bear Collection, Limited Edition or Polo Stadium, we were all over it.

When we'd be out and about with Mom, the Lo Lives would holler at us.

LO LIVES
What-what. Twin-Lo!

MOM
Why are they hollering at you? You better *not* be hanging out with them.

TRISH
We just see them around the neighborhood.
I thought you once said that we should make friends with all sorts of people?

> MOM
>
> All sorts, but not every sort. Don't be
> *too* nice, now. I'm not sure if I like
> those boys.

> NETTE AND TRISH
>
> *Mom!*

Some weekends, Mom would whisk us off into Manhattan to get some education on the other side of the East River. She liked to introduce us to the finer things, even ones we couldn't really afford. We went to Saks Fifth Avenue and explored the makeup section. We went to the Museum of Natural History and gawked at the giant blue whale suspended from the ceiling. We went to Broadway shows and clapped till our hands hurt—then went home and stashed the *Playbills* under our beds as souvenirs. Mom showed us how to be cultured. She was aspirational. Just like the Lo Lives, in a way.

She wanted us to feel like we belonged anywhere and everywhere. Which is why, the summer after we turned seven, before we met the Lo Lives or even rolled around the neighborhood by ourselves, Mom up and announced that we were going to camp. We didn't want to go to camp! We nearly staged a sit-in *and* a boycott. We wanted to hang out with Grandma and go to the grocery store where she'd allow us to pick out anything we'd like and she'd whip it together like she was Mama Lombardi!

> NETTE
>
> But, Mom, it says it's a Jewish summer camp.
> We aren't Jewish, are we?

> MOM
>
> No.

TRISH
So we won't fit in. Why can't we just play
with Grandma?

MOM
You have to go out into the world and make
friends with all sorts of people.

Mom wanted us to be able to groove with anyone. But in the end, she conceded to send us to camp for only half the summer. On the first day, we cried the whole way there.

Fast-forward to the middle of the summer, and we were bawling again. But this time it was because we didn't want to leave!

We ended up loving camp so much—learning to swim, taking field trips to the aquarium, going to Yankees games and every amusement park in the tristate area—we went every summer till we were thirteen.

Over the years we got to know all sorts of kids from Staten Island, New Jersey, and the greater New York metropolitan area. We were among the only black kids at camp, but it didn't feel weird because we didn't really put much stock into what people looked like. We cared more about how people manifested who they were—what they did, how they did it. But this was the first time we were in the serious minority. It was the first time we seemed so conspicuously different, and also the first time we didn't seem different enough. "Your skin is light, you're not really black," the kids would say, or "You don't talk black, you're just like us." We weren't insulted; we just explained to them how our parents came from Jamaica and how not all black people looked or sounded the same.

Meanwhile, we got to know what upper-middle-class white kids did: play jacks, make lanyards, and kick hacky sacks. We had a wild time trying to explain all those things to our neighborhood friends. We were like the Christopher Columbuses of the hood, bringing back foreign objects and strange tales from our voyage to Marine Park.

We liked being emissaries to camp kids as much as we liked being emissaries to neighborhood kids. We'd tell them all about how, back in Ditmas, you can get slammin curry chicken rotis at Topaz or Blue Mountain or Vee's, and customized-with-your-initials gold fronts at the jewelry store on the corner. We learned to translate experiences so the other side could understand more.

As teenagers, we started attending an all-girls Catholic school. All of a sudden we had uniforms and we had to make room for the Holy Spirit at dances with boys. The school had lots of Irish and Italian girls, but very few Jews or blacks, so we got to know another whole slice of the American Pie we hadn't yet sampled. We made friends pretty quickly and got invited back to their houses for Sunday sauce or took joyrides in their parents' cars. Not only did these girls have houses instead of apartments, they had aboveground pools in their backyards. Their fathers worked and their mothers stayed home. Their fathers owned car dealerships, ran event and catering businesses, and had construction companies with their last names in the titles. And they had parties—*everything* was a reason to have a party. Sleepover parties. Holiday parties. Birthday parties. Half-birthday parties. Graduation parties. Sweet sixteen parties. Damn, we had to buy an entire wardrobe just for those sweet sixteen parties, and Tiffany's should've given us stock options: we spent so much money there on Elsa Peretti necklaces that the saleswomen knew our names.

These Catholic school girls wore tight leggings under loose, oversized flannel shirts, and nice boots. They *always* had good boots. And they all smoked Marlboro Lights like they were sponsored, getting paid per puff. Damn, we thought to ourselves: *We are getting schooled in how the other half lives.* We loved the newness of it all.

And then sometimes, when we were juniors or seniors, we'd take our friends with us into the city to go to clubs. Since we had a curfew, we'd slip out after Mom was fast asleep, but these girls had parents who didn't care how late they stayed out. Our high school friends were as amazed that we could get into clubs and knew the DJs as we had been about the backyard pools. Just like at camp, we shared what we had and what we knew, and they did the same.

So by the time we went to college we'd been exposed to lots of different people and we'd started to sense who we were drawn to. When we first pulled up at Skidmore College, we were very aware of our race and our income (or lack thereof). Some of the cars in the parking lot might as well have been made out of bricks of cash! But any insecurities we had began to dissipate as we got to know all the cliques, clubs, and little communities. And we mean all of them! We hung with the pockets of Dominicans and the black kids. We hung out with the artsy kids. We hung out with the L.A. and New York money kids. We hung out with the kids who had been to pretty boarding schools and we hung out with the kids on scholarships. But instead of just hitching ourselves to one of these crews, we started to assemble our own.

We connected with people over music and culture, often with kids who knew New York City, who understood the energy and the excitement, the hustle and the hunger, the thrill and the thrall. We wanted friends who could teach us things—and who also wanted to soak up all the knowledge they could. We sought out friends who wanted to grow and who encouraged us to grow, not people who saw us one way and didn't want us to change. We grew up during the advent of hip-hop, and that sense of mixing and matching, sampling and freestyling, cultural exchange and appropriation led us to think of our social lives in similar terms—we loved the unexpected, the fusion of new and old, the diversity of voices. After all, we came from the Matriarchy—where the motto was "All for one and one for all"—and in our own grown-up lives we've made it a priority to re-create that tight-knit feeling.

So take it from us: there's nothing more important in life than surrounding yourself with people who respect where you've been and where you want to go, people who you can do right by, and who will do right by you. People who will push you to be your best self because you push them to be theirs. Your tribe is your elevation—it ought to lift you up. At the same time, your tribe is your gravity—it ought to keep you grounded. Your tribe can be so many things—if you're willing to double down on it.

Be Active About Your Crew So It Can Activate You

Too many people's social lives just happen to them. The Status Quo conditions you to think that it's really hard to make friends, so you'd better hang on tight to the friends you have. That's not only crazy but also totally inaccurate. Whether you're shy and introverted or love being the life of the party, and whether your typical spot is a quiet coffee shop or a club, you can always find new people who get what you're about.

See, the Status Quo's theory of friendship is **passive accumulation**. This is like those extra blouse buttons that accumulate in that dish on your dresser. You keep them because they are shiny and came with your new outfits—and because you figure they might come in handy someday—but really, they're just sitting there, gathering dust, because you have them and it feels wrong to toss them out. Those buttons are like your college roommate who you bonded with when you were eighteen and feeling homesick, and your college ladies who held your hair back when you drank too much. They're like your best work friend from your first job who stuck up for you that time and your best work friend from your second job who you stuck up for that other time; the girl friend you met through your first boyfriend and the guy friend who used to chill with your second boyfriend. Don't get us wrong: these relationships are all good. Maybe even great. But only if they're still in your life for the right reasons—and serving a purpose.

Sometimes you may find that people you were once close to are no longer supporting your journey. This can be especially true of your high school and college friends. These are friendships that were forged during transitional times, and it's normal to feel close to people when you've been through a lot together. There's power in shared experiences, for sure. But sharing is not always caring. While you may remain friends forever, it's important that these friends allow you to be yourself as you are now, not just take you back to who you were once. Because you may not be who you *were,* and they might not be ready for who you *want to be.* You can't just keep people around you from a vague sense of obligation or guilt, or fear if they can't give you the space to become who you need to be.

That's why our theory of friendship is **deliberate cultivation**. You don't hear much about how you should be deliberate as hell when it comes to friends, but it's one of the things we're the most conscientious about. If you're being vigilant about your skills, your dreams, your work, your time, about what you eat, and how much you go to the gym—then why wouldn't you be *super* vigilant about who you're investing your time in?

People are the best investment in your success, whether personal or professional. No one can go it alone. We all want to share our triumphs, and we all want to feel supported when we get beat. Your crew is like a garden: you need to tend to it and eliminate the weeds, and it'll always give back to you—it'll always be a thing of beauty.

The Status Quo would have you believe that you should always look out for yourself and be wary of opening up to others; it will tell you that if you give, other people will take—and then you'll have nothing left for yourself. There are Takers, for sure, but when you're talking about your crew, it's the people who give *and* take that you should be doubling down on without reservation.

If you're part of a crew, you're woven into the fabric of a great tapestry. You're one cell in a multicell organism, the bass line in a funk song or a violin in the symphony. You are part of something bigger than yourself, which will make you bigger on your own, filling you with purpose. Despite what the Status Quo would have you believe, being needed is extremely gratifying and life-affirming. We all want to be useful to the people we love.

How to Cultivate Your Tribe

Every January we take a trip right around New Year's to a place where we can unwind, warm up, and get ready for another exciting year. Recently, we went to St. Martin, another year we went to Tulum. After we've had a day or two to decompress and soak up the sun (and a night or two to meet people and dance), you'll find us poolside under a big blue-and-white umbrella or beachside under some shady palm trees. We'll have our phones out—and we'll be getting down to business.

We use this time to check in with ourselves and each other about what we want our next year to look like. We always set goals, not resolutions. We're not the United Nations! We share objectives, what we hope to accomplish. And then we talk about how to achieve them. We aim high and get serious about the follow-through.

And then we apply this process to our crew. We each keep running lists of the people we've been hanging out with, so that at the beginning of each year we can take stock of (1) who we've spent a lot of time with, (2) who we haven't seen much of, (3) who we want to seek out, and (4) who we could stand to see less of. We have lots of friends in common, so we cross-check, but we also have people in our lives who are just friends with one of us. We don't share all the things! (But pretty much all the things . . .)

We include our oldest friends as well as our newest peeps. And then we ask ourselves, simply, should we spend more time with this person, or less? Are we doing right by them, are they doing right by us? Are we growing together, or is there a disconnect? We're not voting anyone off the island *Survivor*-style, and this isn't *Mean Girls* either. We're thinking strategically about who we're sharing our best selves with.

It's on you to know who and what you need in your crew. It's also on you to know what your individual friends offer you. All friends are not created equal, and that's a good thing. It's a classic Status Quo myth that every friend needs to be your BFF. Wouldn't it be insane if that were the case? It'd be *way* too intense! We love each other, but we're not looking to duplicate the intensity of our Twinity in *all* our friendships!

We look at our friends in terms of these four categories. Sometimes there's overlap between them, but each group plays a distinct role in your life.

1. YOUR INNER CIRCLE

These are your closest people—siblings, best friends, family, and Aces (more on them in the next chapter). You can call them late at night and text them early in the morning. Their secrets are safe with you, and you'll have their back no matter what (and vice versa).

While we're pretty open and trusting of all new friends, we *really* go all-in for our inner circle. Once we become really close to someone, we treat them like a sister (okay, maybe not a twin, but still, a close sibling). We show up and come out and get behind and cheer on and check in. Just as we take pride in how we do our jobs, we take pride in how we friend. Yes, we just used *friend* as a verb, but it has nothing to do with Facebook. How you *friend* is a skill; it's something you can do well or poorly. When you do it well, not only do you deepen your relationships, but you also empower yourself to be more in control of your life. To *friend* well means you try to help a person become who they were meant to be: you're there to help.

When our friend Talitha's mom had a health scare a few years back, for example, Antoinette happened to be on a business trip to L.A., where Talitha lives with her daughter Selah. We first met Talitha in a work context—she's an agent at the talent agency CAA—but we quickly bonded over goals, passions, and our shared Jamaican roots. We've all been tight ever since. Talitha sent out a group text to let all of us know what had happened with her mom—it's important to share both the good and the bad with your inner circle—and Antoinette replied saying that she was in town and would be happy to pick up Selah from school if Talitha needed the help.

TALITHA

OMG! Are you sure?

NETTE

Hell, yes! I got you. What's the address?

Antoinette canceled her afternoon meeting without thinking twice and was waiting for Selah in the parent pickup line as soon as school got out. Then they went to get pizza and Antoinette took her home to watch *Nailed It*. When Talitha got back late that night,

Antoinette had already put Selah to bed and was reading a magazine on the sofa. The second Talitha walked in she burst into tears.

NETTE
Oh, no, how is your mom?

TALITHA
She's okay! She's gonna be okay. [beat]
I'm just so happy to see you and know that
Selah was taken care of.

Antoinette didn't think she'd done anything special. Probably that's because when we were growing up everyone pitched in to help whenever they could. If Mom was working late, we went to Grandma's, and if Mom needed a weekend to herself, Aunt Monica was happy to have us out to the burbs. This was our model, and it's the kind of support system we try to emulate in our own lives.

When you show up for your people, give without the expectation of getting—they will tend to do the same. You get back what you put in. Some of our friends come from similar backgrounds—big, Matriarchal families—so it's second nature for them, too. At the same time, we have others who didn't have families like ours and aren't necessarily used to the generosity we practice. But when you truly care, people notice. They meet you where you're at.

2. YOUR CREW

Your crew is your broader circle of friends, your extended web of support, the people who cheer you on, who you feel comfortable relying on. You might not see these people every day or every week, but you always have a big smile on your face whenever you do.

For our fortieth birthday party, we planned a big-ass, blowout bash, and the theme was 1970s New York, Studio 54–style. Beforehand, we had a dinner at Omar's private dinner club with forty of our closest friends and family, so all the people we loved were together in one room, chowing down on yummy food. And then it was time for the party—and you know we throw the best parties.

So many people came out to support us! In the low light, the room pulsing with the deep bass of the hip-hop track, we saw our work friends, our high school friends, our college friends; we saw our friends who were spiritual healers and doulas and life coaches; we saw our friends who were photographers and street artists and DJs; we saw our friends who were bankers, venture capitalists, and entrepreneurs. That was our crew.

And all of them, damn near 150 of our people, were dressed to the nines like disco kings and queens, high-collared shirts and short skirts, boas and cummerbunds. We partied all night, like it was 1979—and had the time of our lives.

You can think of your crew as the people who show up to celebrate you, support you, and yes, party with you. And sometimes, these relationships will evolve into something deeper and even more meaningful. We've had lots of friends who started as just members of a crew and eventually became part of our inner circle.

3. YOUR WORK SQUAD

This is who you roll with at work—and after work. These are the people you spend the majority of your days with, the folks you meet through your industry who can relate to what's going on nine to five (or nine to nine). These people are on the front lines with you, fighting the good fight, day in and day out. You get close with these people. You rise up together—and, when you change jobs, you're still tight.

And when you're working around the clock, you need to have someone around who really *gets you*. You need a work wifey.

Your wifey is your lunch buddy, your juice-run partner, the person you roll with to the company party or after-work event and the person you recap with about what went down at the company party or after-work event. Sometimes your work wifeys become part of your crew; they can even wind up as Aces.

One of Antoinette's best friends is Heather, whom she first met when they were producers at *Tyra*. She became Antoinette's work wifey instantly: it was work love at first sight. Heather is super outgoing, mad funny, a real talker. Antoinette and Heather worked hard and inspired each other to be the best—that's what you do with a work wifey. But work wasn't where it ended, they also played hard, too.

Heather gave it her all at the office and at the club. She was ambidextrous like that. After the wrap parties or a night out, she would often spend the night at Antoinette's apartment—only then would she finally run out of steam. It's like she left everything she had in the production office and on the dance floor. She'd walk in the door, make a beeline for the couch, and while Antoinette was mid-sentence recapping the night, Heather closed her eyes and *one* minute later she was knocked out—in full makeup with her gold caged heels and black cap sleeve bodycon dress still on. There was no waking her, so Antoinette would take off her shoes, cover her with a blanket, and say goodnight. It was the least Antoinette could do for her work wifey.

You get real tight with your work squad. After all, you spend most of your waking hours at work, and often, these become the only people who truly know what it's like to *do you*!

4. YOUR BOARD OF ADVISERS

These people are your trusted counsel, the people you consult when you have a big life or work decision. Your board of advisers is made up of anyone whose opinion you respect and value: your Gurus, your Inner Circle, and people in your Crew and your Work Squad—the more people you have on your Board of Advisers, the more people you have to turn to when you need advice. The fact of the matter is, you need lots of people on Team You. You'll need to stack your bench deep if you're gonna be a franchise player.

When you're switching jobs—link up with your Board. When you're having drama in your relationship—link up with your Board. When you're moving apartments or houses—link up with your Board. When Antoinette was trying to decide if she should go full-on bicoastal—since so many of her integrations take place in L.A.—she talked with Cristin, from her Work Squad, who gave her confidence and support and helped her decide. Once she was serious about going ahead with it, Antoinette called her best friends Heather and Talitha for location suggestions in L.A.—Heather sent her various real-estate sites for rentals, and Talitha gave her a tour of her new neighborhood in Larchmont. And Antoinette reached out to Marc, her old work husband (like a work wifey, only a dude) from *Tyra* who now works at *The Talk*, and he was the one who ended up finding her apartment in his building. Your Board can open all kinds of doors for you.

Or take our friend and Boss Lady **Grace Mahary**, one of the most sought-after fashion models working today. She's a beauty inside and out—truly one of a kind. You can see her from a mile away because she's got force—and legs for days! And when she opens her mouth, you're like, *Oh my God, she has a beautiful soul.*

Grace leveraged her power as a model to start Project Tsehigh, a nonprofit that helps bring electricity to villages in her homeland of

Eritrea. This kind of venture is not an easy thing to get off the ground, so she consulted with her Board of Advisers. First she reached out to her friend who worked in grant writing and laid on the questions (*How do we get funding? How do we get people on the ground involved? How do we get people in the diaspora involved?*). Then she hit up her uncle, an engineer who taught her logistics; her cousin, who, Grace told us when we spoke to her, is "a downright boss in finance and corporate structure"; and her friend Joey, who has "a full encyclopedia of knowledge."

Then she reached out to her model friends, photographers, artists, and, she said, "anyone I knew well who could lend their talent and skill to help share this idea." Grace wasn't sure anyone else would be passionate about it the way she was, but it turned out that everyone was excited to get involved and to help. "People have space in their hearts to give," she said to us. "You don't know until you ask."

Soaking up the wisdom of all these people helped Grace transform a vision that could've seemed scary and overwhelming into something attainable. And now, because of the success of Project Tsehigh, hundreds of people in Eritrea have electricity.

Growing and Maintaining Your Crew

Of course, it's not enough to just assemble a kick-ass crew; you have to maintain it, nurture it, keep it fresh. Remember: your crew is like a garden you need to water, weed, and harvest. Friends aren't free. Like all the great things in life, they take work. But being a good friend is some of the most rewarding work you can do, because having a good friend is one of the most rewarding experiences you can have. Trust us! We're best friends and we try to bring that compassion and intensity to all our meaningful relationships.

So does Boss Lady Loren Ridinger, whom we talked about in

chapter 4. Loren goes all-in on the people in her crew—Jennifer Lopez, Alicia Keys, and Eva Longoria. "Jennifer, Alicia, and Eva have always been go-to people for me," Loren told us. "When you have those people around you, who are your number one cheerleaders, you've traded out the negative for the positive. Your tribe knows how you feel. They only want the very best for you."

"Jennifer has this fierce magic that's undeniable," she says. "Alicia is probably the best listener of anyone in the world . . . And Eva is a true girl's girl. She always makes the extra effort." Now, that's a crew!

To help you build out yours, we're gonna start by sharing our givens—truths we hold to be self-evident. These are the precepts we take for granted as we approach all our relationships, and in the long run we've found them to be the reason our crew has remained the powerful force for good that it is in our lives.

1. GIVE WHAT YOU HOPE TO GET

We believe that when it comes to your crew and your people, **you always get back what you put in.** That's our starting point. Now, we know what you're thinking: *What about those times that people have misused my trust, betrayed me, and spoken about me behind my back—after everything I did for them!* The Status Quo loves for you to read too much into a bad experience or two, then extrapolate from that a reason for making your behavior more Status Quo. It's true that sometimes you get burned by not-so-cool people. But we don't think that's a reason to give up on the firepower altogether!

We find that the more open and engaged we are with the people we are close to, the more open and engaged they are with us—and this leads to the deepest, strongest connections. We also find that the energy we invest in people can travel far and wide—and then boomerang back to us in ways we couldn't have predicted. When we like and respect someone, even just a person we meet at a party or a work event, we always look for ways we might be able to help them. Remember what we absorbed from the Matriarchy—that sense of all for one and one for all. It's easy for us to help people who articulate or broadcast *what they're about*. That's what we discovered about our first adult crew at Skidmore—we liked people who were going somewhere and knew it. Whether it's by giving advice, making a referral, or just listening, when people make their passions clear to us, we want to work what we've got to give what we can. Because when you rise to the occasion, when you show up and offer a hand, you elevate yourself and the people around you.

2. BE ACTIVE AND PROACTIVE

Belonging to a good crew is all about being proactive. In the same way that you need to be deliberate, not passive, about cultivating your crew, we wholeheartedly believe: **You gotta be an organizer.** If you want to get together with your crew, don't just wait for your weekly Taco Tuesdays or your monthly Book Club. It's important to change things up and be the organizer of activities. Shared experiences are the best experiences because the memory is exponentially stronger—it lives on through many people.

We love creating shared experiences, especially ones where people we know and people we don't mix and mingle in a real way. Back in 2010, along with our best friend Jen Yu, we came up with the idea for a thing we called Couture, Cocktails, and Cupcakes. All three of us are always looking for opportunities to build tribes around our passion points and combine our interests in fun new ways. So we decided to create one.

We rented out the social space at Tricia's building on West Twenty-Third and invited a number of scrappy and independent entrepreneurs to participate, saying, "We'll give you a big room full of accomplished women with deep networks if you come and do pop-ups." So various hip vendors selling everything from hats to bathing suits showed up, as well as a fancy eyebrow threader and a psychic. Jen worked at Hennessy at the time, so she was able to convince them to donate liquor for the event, and Tricia covered the hors d'oeuvres (yes, there were cupcakes, but also sushi and a sweet bar). Then the three of us invited ten people apiece and told them to each invite five more, so we'd get a great mix of new faces and ones we already knew.

Over 150 smart, stylish, and awesome women came to Couture, Cocktails, and Cupcakes. It was incredible to see how easy it was to get so many cool, inspiring women together in a room. It was our spin on the networking conference. There were no seminars or mo-tivational speakers; women just got to talk and shop and sip signature cocktails. Throughout the evening, people came up to us and told us what a great idea it was and how we should monetize it by tak-ing a cut of all the vendors' profits. But for us it wasn't about making money; it was about making connections.

If you ask us, the best part isn't the event itself; it's the process. For one thing, the planning forces you to think actively and deliberately about the people in your crew—what they have going on and what you have in common. Sure, it takes work, but it's also tons of fun.

Another time, Tricia came up with the idea for Sip Chat Chow. We love food and trying new things, and our friends would always hit us up anyway for restaurant recs when they were traveling or going out, so Tricia started a food blog about the various places we'd eaten—whether in New York, or San Francisco, or L.A. Then Tricia came up with the idea of hosting monthly Sip Chat Chows: evenings where up-and-coming men and women in all fields could get to-gether over great food and drink, each time at a different restaurant. And she encouraged the invitees to hashtag on IG and Facebook to encourage more people to show up each month. She was even able to get celebrities to come—Adrien Brody did one, Taraji Henson another. One actually landed Tricia on the home page of *Huffington Post*, which made even more women want to get involved. Being active and proactive paid off!

3. MAKE NEW MEMORIES

For friendships to last, you gotta keep them fresh. Reminiscing about the good old days is great, but if you're not also making new memories, eventually those old friendships start to wither. We think the best way to make new memories is to find new places.

We like to get out of town in the summertime. August in New York can be brutal—air quality alerts, heat advisories in effect—so we assemble a crew and rent a house out in the Hamptons during the run-up to Labor Day. We love hosting big groups of people! We'll have a group chat going in the weeks before we're set to go, and pretty soon our phones will start blowing up with messages from our crew. It usually starts with someone suggesting something they want to do when we're out there, like go windsurfing. We'll all say, "Hell yesssss!" Then someone else will chime in a day later to say they can't wait to grill fresh fish and drink prosecco. "Hell yesssss!" we'll all say. So not only will the vacation itself bring us all closer together and give us a much-needed break from work, but we'll get these little extra jolts of anticipation and excitement. And then, of course, afterward, we'll be texting for another month about how Jen flirted with the waiter at Nick & Toni's, and how much fun it was to look at the stars on the beach! The memories live on and so the friendships live on, too.

4. SEEK OUT PEOPLE WHO SHARE YOUR VALUES, NOT YOUR OPINIONS

Our last rule of thumb dates all the way back to our Ditmas Park days hanging with the Lo Lives, the Corner Boys, our Catholic School Girls, the Neighbors: when it comes to our crew, we insist on diversity. One of the things that served us the best in our childhood was that we interacted, befriended, learned from, and argued with people from all around. Everyone was interested in different things; they were different colors, their parents had different jobs—and yet we connected, as people, over the things we cared about. Over time, we shared ourselves, they shared their selves, and everyone benefited from the value exchange. **Diversity is a competitive advantage— it gives you the upper hand over the Status Quo.**

This isn't about trying to replicate a United Colors of Benetton ad, it's simply about following the first two precepts we went over: we try to give more than we expect to get, and we orchestrate ways to bring people together. Diversity isn't just a matter of skin color or of where your family comes from; it's a matter of how people think and the perspectives they bring to the table. What we learned from the Brooklyn streets is that when you have a bunch of people with different backgrounds, colors, *and* experiences you tend to learn more about the world, one another, and yourself.

As we always say: never stop learning!

Remember how, back in the day, we told our neighborhood friends all about lanyards and jacks, and we told our Marine Park friends about quarter water and dancehall reggae? And how we loved explaining what was familiar to us *and* what was foreign to us— creating bridges across boroughs, across cultures, and back again? Well, we still love doing that when we mix our friends together.

Except now, we can just put lots of diverse people in a room and watch the bridge building happen.

At our fortieth birthday party, for example, our cousin Michelle, the one who was trained as a lawyer and then became a psychologist, sat across from our friend Latham, who is a doula and wellness expert. Latham talked to Michelle about the book she'd written and the connections she saw between wellness and mental health, and this gave Michelle the idea to take more of a holistic, "360" approach to helping her clients. These are the mash-ups we love. It literally pays to insist on cognitive diversity!

Tricia believes in this principle so much that at Narrative_ she hosts monthly events at the office she calls Nerds, Cool Kids, and Weirdos. She loves to celebrate diverse thinking by bringing in botanists, comedians, DJs, hackers, retail-trend analysts, Broadway show directors—all different sorts of experts who can help the Narrative_ team see things differently. This kind of diversity is an antidote to carpal-tunnel mind and Holland Tunnel vision, because when you're forced to explain what you do or why you do it in a certain way, you can be exposed to fresh approaches and alerted to your own blind spots. And it's not just the team that learns to see the world through another pair of eyes; the guests, too, are introduced to a new line of thinking. When smart people who have expertise in one area get together with smart people who have expertise in another, great things happen.

5. KNOW WHO IS WITH YOU ON YOUR JOURNEY

You don't need everyone in your crew to be on your same path— that'd get as crowded as the Brooklyn-Queens Expressway on a summer Sunday—but you do need them to be on a path that aligns with yours. They need to be on your same journey, and by that we mean to the top! In other words, you need people who will let you grow and go where you need to go and who want to see you follow *your* dreams, not the dreams *they* think you should have. This is a crucial point to keep in mind and can be one of the hardest to implement. It's not easy to pull back from someone, especially an old friend, when you realize they are no longer supporting you on your chosen path.

When Antoinette was just starting out her career in TV, she endured a lot of questioning and pressure from our family about her career choice. Everyone said it was too unstable—and that it wasn't graduate school! It was really hard for her at the time, but Antoinette needed a bit of distance from the family since they weren't yet on board for the journey she was on. Of course, once her career stabilized and she snagged those Emmys, everyone in the family was singing a different tune. And even though Antoinette now knows that the Fam was acting out of love and just trying to protect her, at the time she needed to surround herself with people who understood and supported her dreams.

6. WEED YOUR CREW: KNOW WHEN TO ADJUST EXPECTATIONS AND WHEN TO LET GO

When we're on the beach in January, the waves at our feet, our phone in one hand and a daiquiri in the other, we take stock of our crew so that we can make it stronger. Our goal is always to make our social life richer and more dynamic, and to have it reflect what we hope will come to pass in the year ahead. So when we go through the list of people we've kept over the past year and talk about what the state of the friendship is, we keep a few things in mind about what we want our crew to be—and about what we *don't* want our crew to be.

We like our crew responsive. Friends show up for friends. We know that we tend to give a lot in all our relationships—that's the way we were raised—so we don't necessarily expect a full return from everyone. That said, the people we keep the closest are all givers, and that makes it super easy to ask them for help. Givers are those people who break their backs for you—who put their own lives on hold to help you out. They are people who are attuned to when you need them, who are ready to spring into action when they can. They are people who root for you when you need support and who anticipate ways they can help you on your journey, even if it's something as simple as sending you an encouraging text at the right time.

But, inevitably, people will pop up in your crew who take more than they give. Sometimes you can have a conversation with that person about what is and isn't working in the friendship; other times you may realize that this person just doesn't belong in your life.

When we realize certain friends are always hitting us up for professional help or referrals but are rarely coming through for us when we celebrate an accomplishment or host an event, we just start to downgrade the energy we invest in them. We'll still see those fair-weather friends and have a drink and catch up. It's still fun to see them—maybe they're funny, or maybe they tell good stories. We have a friend who could be a stand-up comic she's so hilarious. She always cuts right to the bone when she's making fun of things. We listen, we laugh. At the same time, she is difficult to relax with or have a long talk with, because she's usually attacking or criticizing things. That's just her mode. We love her eye and her sharp wit, but we just find that we don't gravitate in the long run to people grooving on that wavelength.

We've learned to appreciate what to expect and what *not* to expect from a friend like this. We are happy to see her out and about, but we don't count on her for the important exchanges that we view as integral to our real and deep relationships.

We have another friend who tends to be all doom and gloom. There's always *something* going on for her that keeps her troubled. We're not unsympathetic, but it's like she's always tromping through quicksand—and pulling us down with her. That's just how she is, even if things are going well. We've been friends with her for years, and we always want to support her because we've been through a lot, but we also know that expecting her to change her personality isn't really in the cards. So if we are planning to have a relaxing Sunday brunch, we might not invite her, but we'll chat with her if we see her at a screening for a new show or film and have a great time.

Sometimes when a friend isn't living up to your expectations, you need to take a look at your expectations. Are you holding your breath waiting for this friend to deliver something she can't? If you keep inviting someone to events and activities and she keeps not showing up, then maybe you shouldn't expect her to show up when it really counts. In other words, you need to **know your friend's role.** We have lots of friends whom we consider social friends—we love to spend time with them when we run into them, but we don't look to them when we need advice or real talk. It's important to know where your friends stand—that's the point of making the list.

But when you realize that someone in your crew is constantly sucking up your time, energy, and goodwill without doing any replenishing, you need to downgrade the role that friend plays in your life—or maybe cut her loose entirely. There are various names for these kinds of people—Energy Vampires is a popular one—but we just call them Takers. The point is: **your people need to give you energy, not drain it.**

It can be hard to scale back on a friendship, even with a Taker. You feel guilty, selfish, maybe even straight-up cruel. But here's the thing: in situations like these, cutting someone loose is actually the kinder thing to do. Why? Because if a friend is always asking for help, or always coming to you with her problems, or always talking about herself, eventually you'll start to resent her, and avoid being around her—only she won't have any idea why. Ghosting a friend is a lot more hurtful than having an honest conversation about why the friendship is no longer working for you.

That's why you should begin the process of divestment *before* you get to resentment. Sometimes during our January check-in, maybe when the waiter in the crisp white shirt approaches our lounge chairs with another fancy cocktail in hand, we'll discover that some newer friends in our wider circle are actually becoming people we want to bring closer into our crew! Like when we met this husband-and-wife team—and they really are like a team—at an opening for a restaurant a few years back and just really hit it off with them. He's a very chill I-banker and she's a model-turned–hospitality exec, and they revel in the New York City nightlife. They're people who really love to take advantage of what the world has to offer and share those experiences with others. For example, every Thursday they plan a dinner at a different restaurant and invite ten people, often people who don't know each other. Those kinds of things can sometimes be awkward and forced, but somehow with this couple they never are.

When Antoinette threw Tricia a surprise launch party for Narrative_, she invited them, and not only did they come out and celebrate—they also asked if they could show up early to help out. Since then, they've become core members of our crew: people we've started to count on. They give more than they expect to get, they love bringing interesting people together, and they share our value of friendship and learning new things. When you meet someone you connect with, you shouldn't hesitate to bring them into the fold.

That's the great thing about a crew! It's alive, full of energy—and you are in control of it. Don't let the Status Quo make you believe that you're at the mercy of your past. You need to be edging into the future with a crew that'll help you do it.

Remember: don't inherit, build. We still approach the building of our crew the way we did back on the streets of Brooklyn. There are so many people we can chat with, so many groups we can plug into, so many conversations we can partake in, so much to learn about! This is the world of the mix and mingle, the give and the get, the learn and teach. So tend to your crew, watch it grow, and reap the rewards!

On the Download

Choose deliberate cultivation over passive accumulation.
You gotta stay on top of your crew like it's your job. They pick you up, have your back, and help you fly—so you'd better be vigilant about who you let in.

You always get back what you put in.
The more you give, the more you get. When you're open, giving, and generous, opportunities come to you. The Status Quo tells us we should be hustling only for ourselves, but it's good to remember how much small actions for others can lift us up.

You gotta be an organizer.
Don't *wait* for things to happen *to* you. *Make* things happen *for* you. Set aside time every week to plan social activities for the next week, the next month, and the next month after that. Then invite your crew.

Diversity is a competitive advantage—it gives you the upper hand over the Status Quo.
It's important to find people you connect with, but that doesn't mean they all need to act, dress, or look like you. In fact, they shouldn't! Keep your crew diverse.

Know each friend's role.
Every friend plays a different role in the movie of your life. Be aware of your friends' strengths and weaknesses; no one is perfect. It's okay to have certain friends you expect only certain things from, and do only certain things with. You can't be everything to everyone, so you can't expect others to be either.

Your people need to give you energy, not sap it.
You happily give to your crew, but don't go all-in on people who constantly need things from you, or who pop up in your life only when things aren't going well for them. True friends share both victories and defeats.

chapter seven

Don't Just Be About Number 1, Get a Number 2

Growing up, we did everything together. If there was one of us, there were two of us. We were so tight we thought "being alone" meant being with each other. Trish and Nette. Nette and Trish. We ate together, brushed our teeth together, made friends together, shopped together, listened to music together. One of us knew what the other was thinking before she said it—sometimes even before she thought it.

We also fought with each other. A lot.

Boy, we fought like welterweights vying for the championship—and the gloves came off. We made fun of each other, bit each other, sat on each other; we pulled hair, pinched arms, punched legs; we poked, tripped, and cried. We chased each other around the house, shouting and yelling. It was mayhem.

MOM
Quiet down now! You both are lunatics!

NETTE

Give it back to me!

TRISH

Look at her! [*hands on hips*] *Give it back to me!*

NETTE

Don't imitate me; I'll pull your hair right out of your head.

TRISH

Okay, okay. [*hands on hips*] *I'll pull your hair right out of your head.*

MOM

Someone is going to end up seriously hurt . . . If you won't listen to me I will call the police on both of you! Stop it!

After particularly bad fights, Mom would separate us, forcibly. She would lock one of us in our room and would tell the other to sit in the hallway till we stopped acting like lunatics. (Mom was always calling us lunatics.) And each time, we both would seethe for a few minutes, and then we *really* started acting like lunatics, because we got super lonely! Just like that, the punches that had been thrown, and our reasons for throwing them, faded into the past, and we wanted to be friends again. We'd both make our way to the closed door to stick our hands underneath and touch the tips of the other's fingers. We could never stay angry at each other for very long—and always wanted to feel connected.

One time when we were nine years old, while Mom was driving us to go hang at Aunt Monica's, we started fighting in the backseat over a book. Nette would read a page, then Trish would snatch it away— back and forth, with lots of shrieking and screaming. This started about as soon as we got on the Long Island Expressway, meaning there was an hour and a half to go. Mom shouted at us to stop, but we didn't listen.

> **MOM**
> You're distracting me. Do you want us to get in an accident?

> **NETTE**
> You *always* boss me around, Trish. Gimme the book!

> **TRISH**
> Nah, it's mine.

> **MOM**
> I'm going to put you two out on the road!

> **NETTE**
> Give it back!

> **TRISH**
> Hey, why did we stop?

> **MOM**
> Get out of the car!

Shit, she was serious. We stopped fighting immediately and stepped out of the car. Mom reached back, closed the door, and drove off.

No joke—she left us standing there, on the side of the road, traffic whizzing by. We were *all alone*! We started crying and held each other and reassured each other that it was gonna be okay because at least we had each other. After about five minutes, Mom turned back up, but the message got through loud and clear: Mom was not messing around.

Another time, we were yelling at each other about *something* when we heard a knock at the door—one of those hard knocks, knuckles on metal. We went to answer it. Two tall men in full-on uniform were in the doorway.

Mom had called our bluff; she'd called the cops on us!

Officer Cooper and Officer Washington asked us what was going on—why we were fighting, who started it; they wanted *the truth*, they informed us. We joined hands and started pleading for mercy—not for ourselves, but for fear that the other would be taken away.

Eventually, the cops said they weren't going to arrest anyone and told us to mind our mother. We closed the door behind them and breathed a sigh of relief.

"Mom is crazy!" we both said in unison.

And then we both noticed we were still holding hands.

That's really how it's always been for us—we've always held the other's hand. Through the childhood squabbles, the adolescent angst, we always felt more whole together than we did when we were apart.

No doubt, growing up as twins gave us a unique perspective on friendship. It taught us what it means to truly have another person's back. And, yes, sometimes shit got intense. We fought each other, for sure, and we still fight, though much less. But for every time we've fought *with* each other, there are probably ten times that we fought *for* the other. That's how it goes, too.

We like to think of ourselves as a pair of Aces: alone we're just two cards; together, we make a damn good hand. In the previous chapter, where we talked about the groups of people in your Tribe, we deliberately left out one important piece—and that's your Ace or Aces, those people you can always go all-in with, you always double down on, and you always return to. These are your ride or dies. Having a partner in crime is essential for your long-term success, and that's why we want to devote a whole chapter to Aces.

But let us be clear. An Ace doesn't need to be someone who shares your DNA. Not at all. Whether it's your cousin or your work wifey or your childhood BFF, your Ace is that one other person you can turn to in your worst moments and best ones—to lift you out from the depths of despair and of self-doubt and to celebrate with you when you're on top of the world. An Ace gives you confidence when your tank is empty, an Ace comes through in the clutch, an Ace rides shotgun when you need to drive. Every Boss Lady needs to have at least one Ace up her sleeve.

As Aces, we are each other's built-ins. We got a problem? We call the other. We got good news? We call the other. We see something funny and want to make the other laugh? We text the other. We are each other's Ace. Never give up, never give in.

That is, we never allow the *other* to give up or give in. Ever since we were kids, we pushed each other to excel—study hard, play hard, and get back up quickly when one of us fell down. Hell, there are times when each of us will get blue or bummed out about something and feel like it's the end of the world. Sometimes Nette will get down on herself about something she's doing in a relationship, or she'll get worried about her job, and Tricia will raise her up and talk some sense into her. Other times, Tricia will be facing a big challenge at work, or be confused about an interaction she had with one of her girlfriends, and Nette will swoop in to put things in perspective.

Your Ace is also the one person in your life you can count on to tell you the hard truth, call you on your shit, and lay on the tough love. The one person who calls it like she sees it—the good, the bad, and the ugly. We all have moments when we sabotage ourselves through self-doubt, or set ourselves up to fail with unreal expectations, or whip ourselves up into a hot temper when what we really need is cool calculation and composure. And we all have moments when we don't even realize we're doing any of those things! That's where your Ace comes in. Your Ace is likely to give you advice even if you don't ask for it, like the time Talitha called Tricia out for working too much and for talking about her work too much.

An Ace holds your ground when you're stumbling backward. An Ace takes your hand when you're fumbling in the dark. An Ace sits you down and sets you straight when you're acting turned around. An Ace takes away your phone when you're threatening to call your ex to ask him why you broke up in the first place. An Ace is like another pair of eyes; when you are having trouble seeing something clearly, you can count on an Ace to bring a pair of binoculars.

Give Confidence, Get Confidence

Late in the spring semester of our sophomore year in college, Susan, one of the women who worked in the Skidmore dining hall who we used to chat with while waiting on line at the pasta station, gave Antoinette an article she'd clipped out of the *New York Post*. It was about a restaurant called Twins that was opening that summer on Eighty-Ninth and Second back in the city. Apparently, it was owned by twins, and only twins were going to work there. Susan thought we *had* to apply. We both had already arranged nonpaying three-day-a-week internships for ourselves—Tricia at an ad agency, Antoinette with NBC News—but Antoinette figured that this restaurant gig could be a great way to make some much-needed cash on the side, *if* we could score ourselves jobs there. Tricia was skeptical.

> **TRISH**
> If it's in the paper, they've probably already got all their hires.

> **NETTE**
> Well, it wouldn't hurt to try. We should at least check the place out.

TRISH
What do we even know about waiting tables?

NETTE
What's there to know? There's a table—then
you wait!

Once we got back home to the city and settled in for the summer, Antoinette called the restaurant. It was owned by two women—twins!—who said they'd already seen a lot of applicants but agreed to do one final interview if we could hustle uptown right then and there. Tricia was sure there was no way they'd hire us because we had no experience—fair enough—but Antoinette wouldn't take no for an answer. We did a lightning-quick hair and makeup check, put on matching skirts and blouses, sprinted to the Q train, and made it there in record time.

Antoinette took the lead in pitching us, and, well, she basically crushed it. The owners were like, "Terrific. We'd like you to join the team. What do you want to do?" That's when Antoinette remembered that we didn't know how to make a martini or even a virgin Shirley Temple and almost started to panic. But she pulled herself together and replied with great poise, "We feel our interpersonal skills would be best suited for hosting."

One owner said, "Good. You start tomorrow night."

And that was that.

We couldn't believe our luck! Now we could earn experience from our internships during the day *and* money working at the restaurant at night. And that's what we did. Three times a week, we drove into the city at 7 a.m. in our red Toyota Tercel and got off work at 5 p.m. Then we'd meet up, drive uptown to the restaurant, work the shift till 1 a.m., and then head back to Brooklyn, where we were living at home with Mom. We were in bed by 2 a.m. and up and at it again at 6. It was hard work, but we loved every minute of it. And if it hadn't been for Antoinette's fearless confidence, we never would've even called up that restaurant in the first place. Where Tricia wanted to hold back, Antoinette moved us both forward.

And she was just getting started.

Since the restaurant Twins was quite a novelty—*everyone* who worked there was a twin—it attracted a decent amount of local news buzz. As hosts, we stood out front, so we were often the first employees any reporter doing a story would see. We got featured in a few newspaper articles and appeared on *Good Day New York*. One evening, during a lull in the foot traffic, Antoinette had an idea.

> **NETTE**
> We're getting featured and people want to take pictures of us being twins, right?

> **TRISH**
> Right.

> **NETTE**
> But it's at this restaurant, Twins, right?

> **TRISH**
> Right.

> **NETTE**
> So why don't we cut out the middleman, book some shit ourselves?

> **TRISH**
> Like *modeling*?

> **NETTE**
> Yeah, ads and editorials. Why's that *so* crazy?

> **TRISH**
> We're short. And aren't we too old? We're not
> models. We're not *model hot.*

> **NETTE**
> That shit doesn't matter. And we may not be
> *model*-model hot, but we're *twin*-model hot.
> We gotta work this!

Tricia wasn't feeling it, so Antoinette felt it for the both of us. She had the confidence and she shared it. Won over by Antoinette's fearlessness, Tricia agreed to give it a try.

At that point we were working five nights a week at Twins and three weekdays at our internships, so we devoted the other two weekdays to going on auditions and go-sees. Sometimes we got there and waited in line, only to be told they didn't need us. Other times we waited in line, got seen for two seconds, only to be told they didn't need us. It was demoralizing!

Tricia was losing the faith after a week or two—so Antoinette doubled down on hers. The thing was: Antoinette didn't *feel* any more intrinsically optimistic than Tricia. It *was* demoralizing! We hadn't scored a single gig! And take it from us, waiting in line for an hour just to have some judgmental casting director look you up and down and send you home can *really* take the wind out of your sails. But when Antoinette saw how dejected *Tricia* was getting, she knew she had to do something about it. In good times and bad, that's what you gotta do: **be the person your Ace needs you to be.**

Antoinette knew that the Status Quo wanted us to throw in the towel. She knew that the Status Quo would say: *Stay in your lane, quit when it's hard, know your limits.* But Antoinette wasn't having any of it. She told herself: *We haven't reached our limits, nothing great is easy, and this IS our lane—dammit.* Antoinette knew that this moment demanded that she be an Ace. She knew she needed to go all-in—for both of us.

The very next go-see we went to, we didn't get seen. At the next one, they saw us and didn't want us. But the following week, we booked our first editorial for a feature about makeup habits. We'd done it! And here's the thing about breaking into a new space—once you're in the door, you're *in*. Once we booked one gig, we made damn sure whoever we were meeting with knew we were now in the game.

That summer we ended up booking a good number of editorials and even made it to the final round for a national TV ad campaign for a shampoo brand. Naturally, we let the owners at Twins know that two of their employees were booking gigs. We were practically celebrities, we thought to ourselves; they should be proud that we worked there. (They didn't give us the raise we wanted, but it was worth a try.) Then school started back up, so we drove up to Skidmore and threw ourselves into our studies and working at the library—until one day we got a call.

It was Samantha Fray from *20/20*. Calling from Barbara Walters's office. She'd gotten our names from the owners of Twins, who'd said we'd be great for a feature they were doing on beauty products and (big surprise!) twins.

We couldn't get the words "Hell yes" out fast enough, and a few weeks later they flew us back to New York to do a "Day in the Life" piece. Later in the year, we booked a shoot for *McCall's*. Then a spread in *Fitness* magazine. And we didn't even work out! And then, the following year, we got to do an editorial spread in *Oprah* magazine! Oprah!

We had opened up a completely new White Space for ourselves— and it was because Antoinette pushed Tricia to keep going. That's what Aces do for each other—ride or die, in good times and bad, through thick and thin, hell or high water. A lot of the time, that means letting your Ace borrow some of the extra confidence you have in them. Because the great thing about lending confidence is that it always gets repaid—with interest.

The bottom line is this: **to have an Ace, you need to be an Ace.** It's a feedback loop that gains in intensity with each go-around. The more confidence and love you give to others, the more confidence and love you will get back—and the more you get back, the more you will have and give to yourself. That's how having an Ace can amplify your powers, exponentially.

It Pays to Have an Ace Up Your Sleeve

Not long after that shoot, we each got a separate call from a casting director who needed women for a Levi's commercial, and to our surprise, they weren't even looking for twins! It was the first audition we'd ever done without the other. We were both kind of nervous, but we just tried to be ourselves.

The following Tuesday, Tricia's phone rang. It was the director, calling to tell her that she'd got it! She'd booked the Levi's campaign— and, as the director very deliberately added, it was *national*. The casting director said the word *national* all velvety-like, the way airline people say *first class* and waiters say *truffle oil*. Tricia got the message: That's the big time! Right away, she thought to herself: *I can't believe we did it!*

And then she realized that this time we weren't a *we*. The director had mentioned only her name. What about Antoinette? She decided to wait a minute to call Nette and find out if she'd gotten the call, but since she couldn't really contain her excitement, she called Mom. Mom hadn't heard from Antoinette yet—so they three-wayed her.

> TRISH
>
> Nette, did anyone call you from the Levi's
> shoot?

> NETTE
>
> No, why?

Here's what was going through our heads in the five seconds of silence that ensued:

> TRISH
>
> *Oh, no, I've got this great news that I want*
> *to share with my Ace, but it's gonna be hard*
> *for her to hear if she didn't get the callback,*
> *too. Do I act sad? Or do I just be who I am, be*
> *happy, and tell her what happened? What would*
> *Antoinette do if the roles were reversed?*

> NETTE
>
> *Oh, wow, she got the callback! That's great.*
> *I don't want to ruin this for her, but, I mean,*
> *why didn't I get one too? Do I just fake it and*
> *seem extremely excited? Or do I just be who I*
> *am, tell her I'm a little disappointed? What*
> *would Tricia do if the roles were reversed?*

At that moment, Antoinette had to get off the phone—she was getting an incoming call from an unknown number. It turned out to be the director calling with the exact same news he'd given Tricia—once again stressing *national* the way jewelers say *24-karat* and used car salesmen say *zero down for thirty-six months*.

We'd both made it together—but separately.

When Antoinette called Tricia back and told her, Tricia experienced the same joy she'd felt earlier, but this time it was squared, exponential. We were both so happy—and relieved—we started screaming like the couple of lunatics Mom had accused us of being as kids.

But here's the thing: we'd also been prepared to anticipate the other's needs if things had gone the other way. We each tried to be present and prioritize what the other was gonna feel. We were able to put our own feelings aside and make room for the other's—and that brought us even closer.

The Levi's spot was slated for two days of filming. They had initially thought they were going to use us separately, but when they saw us together they realized they needed to have us featured side by side. And take it from us: there's no magic like getting to share a golden moment with your Ace.

Then one day in early November, we got word on the air date of the commercial. It could not have been better: Thanksgiving Day, right in the middle of the football game. (Don't ask us who was playing.) You can bet our whole family gathered for the feast—we all crowded around Grandma's bubble TV, waiting for those thirty seconds of glory. Even our family, which takes a dim view generally of accomplishments that don't require a master's or a PhD, was proud to see us representing our Jamaican heritage on the—ahem—*national* stage.

The commercial went into heavy rotation, and the week after Thanksgiving we opened up the mailbox. There were envelopes addressed to each of us. We opened them simultaneously—they were residual checks. Seven thousand dollars apiece! Our jaws hit the floor. We'd already been paid a few thousand dollars for the two-day shoot, but now that the ads were airing we got a fee every time. And those small fees, over the course of a few months, became fat-ass checks. That Christmas it snowed a lot—a steady flurry of residual checks falling from the sky.

Suddenly, the door to a whole new world opened up, because we could finally afford to buy a key to it: we could get our own place in Manhattan, buy our own furniture, and even pay off our student loans. This was our first step toward starting our new lives as working women. We were on our own, and we would write our own rules. Our new apartment was on Gold Street, which couldn't have been any more apt. Like solid gold: that's how we felt exactly.

The first night we spent in our own apartment together was a dream come true. And the best part? All of it had been underwritten by our Twinity, our relationship—also those fat residual checks—but mostly our relationship. We'd put our faith in the other, our confidence in the other; we'd pushed each other, challenged each other; and now we were a pair of Aces in the big city at the start of our great adventure.

We were really proud of ourselves for taking this side hustle as far as we did—*national,* that is—but it was time to retire from the modeling game. We'd proven to ourselves that we could do it, and that was cool. But modeling was never our North Star. It was always just a means to an end: a way to bank enough cash to launch us on that longer journey in pursuit of our dreams. Now Antoinette needed to chase that producer title, and Tricia needed to lock down some big accounts. We were intent on carrying out the New American Hustle. Together. That's what the Long Game is all about.

A Pair of Aces Come in All Different Suits

Thelma and Louise. Bonnie and Clyde. Puff and Biggie (RIP). Laverne and Shirley. Run and DMC. John and Paul. Batman and Robin. Lucy and Ethel. Havoc and Prodigy (RIP). Talib and Mos Def. That's what we call proof that together, Aces can rock anything. That's because Aces complement each other in big and small ways. We've always been amazed and inspired by what the other can do—Tricia could never do what Antoinette does, and Antoinette could never do what Tricia does. We're so alike, yet we're in awe of our differences. Many of Tricia's strengths are Antoinette's weaknesses, and many of Tricia's weaknesses are Antoinette's strengths.

By natural constitution, Tricia is more assertive than Antoinette. She tends to push a little harder for the things she wants. This tendency leads her to think a little more ambitiously. But from years of watching Tricia advocate for herself, Antoinette learned how sometimes you need to throw your weight around and make some noise when you need or want something. She learned how to channel Tricia in this way, and eventually it became second nature.

On the flip side, Tricia can be more impulsive, which can get her into trouble. Antoinette, on the other hand, really thinks things through before she commits. From observing the way Antoinette always looks before she leaps, over time Tricia eventually learned to do the same.

The point is: we complement each other! We balance the other out. We learn from each other's mistakes and victories. This isn't just a twin thing: all Aces can act as your personal supermodels of skills, and when you have a person in your life who's always trying to help you become a better version of yourself, you can learn anything.

You Need an Ace in the Work Space

In work, just as in life: it pays to have an Ace by your side.

What they don't tell you when you start out in the workplace is that you actually have *two* jobs that require 100 percent of your attention. First off, you have whatever it says in your job description—whether that's answering phones, making mock-ups, pitching brands, taking photographs, playing your instrument, writing copy, or running social media. Those are things you are getting paid for—the things you have to do to earn that check at the end of the month. You need to give them 100 percent.

At the same time, no matter what you do or where you work, you also have a second job: dealing with other people. In all jobs, every job, you have to work with people, answer to people, and speak for people. You're dealing with people all the time. You've got colleagues, bosses, and clients, all making competing demands on your time and your attention. Meanwhile, they aren't thinking about your time and attention because they are too busy worrying about the demands that other people are putting on theirs. It's hella stressful.

That's where your Ace comes in. Your Ace at work is the person you turn to when it all gets to be too much: your work husband or work wifey. This is different from a guru or a mentor; it's the person you commiserate with about the confusing office politics, or bitch to when one of those bosses or colleagues or clients leads you to question your sanity and every decision you've ever made to lead you to this one moment. Your Ace at work is the person you grab leafy-green salads with on your lunch break and ice-cold martinis with at happy hour o'clock. It's someone you can trust, someone who supports you (and whom you support), someone you can talk to about problems and strategize with about solutions, someone who knows you well enough to see when something's going on.

When Tricia started work at Emmis, she was by far the youngest person on the team, and it was a little hard for her to find her people or know what to bond with people about. But soon enough, by shooting the shit enough, she discovered that Lisa, who was a few years older, was into some of the same nightspots. From there, they hit it off. Lisa was tall, with long brown hair, a curvy figure, and a beaming personality. And like Tricia, Lisa was way into the Four Fs: Friends, Family, Food, and Friday night partying. By hanging out after hours, they built up a solid bond and started to turn to each other during work hours if either one needed advice or help. Lisa also taught Tricia the art of lunching. The world changed on or about the day of that first lunch in spring 2000. Up until that point, Tricia stepped out to get food to bring back to her desk or took a sandwich to the park. Lisa wasn't having any of it—not a single sad desk salad. She'd insist they eat out *at least* a few times a week— Snack Taverna, Blue Ribbon, Bar Pitti. At lunch they talked about work to blow off steam, or they struck up conversations with other patrons. Lisa made working at Emmis fun, because Tricia now had an ally she could rely on.

When Antoinette arrived at *Montel,* she saw there was an amazingly tight-knit team of people who had been at the show for years— which is rare in TV, where there's lots of turnover. She liked the camaraderie, but it took a while for her to earn her stripes and acceptance into the crew. She eventually bonded with two coworkers who soon enough became her Aces. The first was Susan, who was already a producer, the only other African American on the show. She was Jamaican, too, so they shared some common cultural touch-points. Antoinette knew she could turn to Susan in a pinch if she was unsure about a booking or wanted advice on how to position herself for a promotion. That early support and inspiration helped her acclimate and ground-built the confidence she needed to thrive in the high-pressure environment.

Her other Ace was Melissa, who was also just starting out at the bottom rung of the ladder. Melissa provided a little yin to Antoinette's yang: for one thing, Melissa was *super* confident. She rocked her confidence like it was a new pair of heels. Antoinette would get freaked out when she needed to pitch the EPs, but Melissa just walked into rooms and pitched like Pedro Martínez. She had nerves like cold steel. Antoinette watched and studied how she plowed through obstacles. It wasn't that Melissa was without fear—no one is—but Melissa just didn't give a fuck about it. By watching Melissa act fearlessly, Antoinette saw how she too could act fearlessly.

At the same time, when Antoinette was feeling down, Melissa would always light up the room and lighten the mood—she was funny as hell! Melissa had this buoyant and lively energy, and she understood intuitively that **when your Ace is in the darkness, give her light.**

But as we said earlier, even the baddest of Boss Ladies has her weaknesses, and Melissa's was that her desk looked like it had been hit by a hurricane. She didn't understand the benefit of a well-ordered workspace until Antoinette came along with the mantra of everything in its place. From her, Melissa learned how being organized not only helps you find things faster but can help you think more clearly.

Antoinette and Melissa confided in each other and rooted for each other, and when they eventually both got promoted to producer, they were able to share that pride, the excitement, and the celebratory champagne, of course, with each other.

Grow Together and Know When to Let Go

One of the best parts about having an Ace is the joy of growing up together. We aren't talking literally, the way we grew up together in Ditmas Park; we mean the ongoing process of learning, maturing, and gaining perspective that happens as you get older. Having an Ace up your sleeve can accelerate this growth—especially when it comes to your career.

Take Ali Kriegsman and Alana Branston, cofounders of Bulletin. They met as seatmates when they were working at the content marketing start-up Contently and they hit it off. Ultimately, they weren't super content there, so they decided to collaborate on a side hustle.

Soon they were working nights and weekends trying to get their idea for a cool, shoppable Etsy platform off the ground. That idea evolved over time into Bulletin, a new form of retail store that provides up-and-coming female-led brands with new opportunities to get their products seen online and in brick-and-mortar stores.

"I'm able to believe in myself," Ali told us, "because Alana is so supportive. At the flagship store in New York we launched, I had very little to do with it. Alana was like a wizard . . . Every uphill battle that she dominates, I gain confidence." That's how Aces inspire and feed off each other. As Alana told us, "It was always a divide-and-conquer mentality. The roles are always evolving. When it was just the two of us, I was building up the site, Ali was talking to the brands. Now we have eleven women in corporate and twenty-five women in retail, our roles keep changing. Whatever the business needs, we give to it. And we're able to do that because we have each other." Ali and Alana are Boss Ladies and Aces who have led their business fearlessly—and they've also given over 150 female entrepreneurs the chance to live their dreams.

At the same time, Aces can grow apart—and that's okay, too. When you've known someone for a long time, it's natural that you may eventually begin to veer off into trajectories that are no longer parallel. The Status Quo would have you believe that all endings are (1) bad and (2) messy. Not so. Endings can be (1) sad and (2) difficult, but they can also be the beginning of something new and exciting. Take it from us.

After two years of living on Gold Street—the apartment made possible by our modeling hustle—we moved into a dope spot on Sixteenth between Fifth and Sixth. We didn't know it at the time, but this was going to be the last place we shared together.

This was around when Tricia had started to crush it at Emmis, while Antoinette was marching her way up to a producer at *Montel*—

long-ass hours, little pay. Since Antoinette wasn't making much bank at the time, Tricia covered most of the rent. That's how we roll—when one of us is flush, the other is, too.

We were each so involved with our jobs, we didn't see each other very much during the workweeks, but when the weekend rolled around we were back to our old hijinks. We worked hard, then we played hard. We went out on Friday nights, to a club or a restaurant opening, where we danced and ate like queens, and then we got up early on Saturdays—because we never wanted to waste a weekend day. We'd read the glossy magazines over each other's shoulders while getting a mani/pedi (taupe, burgundy) and accompanied the other on her errands: to the tailor (we were always getting dresses and blouses tailored), to drop off a pair of heels at the shoe repair (we were always, for some reason, getting our shoes repaired), et cetera. We'd hit up our friend Amanda to get brunch, then we'd set out to explore the city, walking down to Nolita and SoHo, looking at the elaborate window displays of the boutiques, ducking in to sample sales, getting ice cream or coffee when we started feeling undercaffeinated or hangry.

Around this time, Tricia had started to seriously date Kris. He was a hottie and had mad swag. They met at a bar lounge called the Rubber Monkey, when one of Kris's friends came up to Tricia saying he was a twin, too; he was seriously working his game. As soon as it became clear to him that Tricia wasn't going for him, he called Kris over. Tricia was like, *Oh, he's cute.* At 3 a.m. they exchanged phone numbers, and Tricia hopped in a cab to go home. As the taxi sped away, her phone rang: it was Kris, calling to make sure she gave him the right number. They went on their first date two days later.

From the beginning, Kris was different from all the boyfriends to come before him. For one thing, he understood and respected our

Twinity. He always made Antoinette feel welcome. When Kris took Tricia shopping during their first Christmas as a couple, Tricia picked out a Chanel bag. "*Oh*, that's nice," he said. "I'll get Antoinette one, too." That pretty much sealed the deal: he knew what was up. As Tricia was throwing herself into the new relationship, Antoinette was throwing herself into work—sleeping at the office on that raggedy-ass carpet under her desk, writing scripts with sleepy eyes, and stressing about work for the few hours when she wasn't actually *at* work.

Eventually, Tricia and Kris decided it was time to take their relationship to the Next Level: They were moving in together. Tricia had never lived with a boyfriend before, and she was excited. But she was always nervous about telling Antoinette—especially since it made the most amount of sense for Kris to move into the place Tricia and Antoinette had been living in (no way they were moving into his 1BR bachelor pad). Finally, one night, Tricia bit the bullet.

> **TRISH**
> So, I've got something to tell you. Kris and I are going to Sweden to see his grandfather.

> **NETTE**
> So cool! Is it going to be freezing there?

> **TRISH**
> And something else. Kris and I decided to move in together.

> **NETTE**
> Wait, what?

> **TRISH**
> And he's gonna move in here.

> **NETTE**
> So, so, so—what's going to happen to me?

Antoinette had known that Tricia and Kris were getting really serious, and a part of her had suspected that they'd move in together eventually—but that was not the part of her that was now bursting into tears. She'd lived with Tricia her whole life! It felt like she was losing her sister, her Ace—and her apartment, all at the same time.

Tricia had anticipated that this news was gonna hit hard. She knew she was putting an end to an era—she felt sad, too, and more than a little bit guilty. So she'd already picked out and paid for the first and last months' rent and the security deposit for an apartment for Antoinette—*rent-stabilized*—around the corner, on Fifteenth and Fifth.

Tricia hugged Antoinette. "Let's go look at the apartment," Tricia said.

Antoinette started to feel a little better as she walked down the sidewalk, feeling the wind on her cheeks. She began to think that maybe she could handle this, maybe this was a good thing. Of course for Tricia and Kris—but her, too.

Then she walked into the apartment. Tricia had failed to mention that the reason the apartment was affordable was that it hadn't been renovated in two thousand years—and apparently had been previously inhabited by a hoarder with the ugliest cream-colored wall-to-wall carpet that we (or anyone) had ever seen. Antoinette started to cry again. But this time the tears were shorter-lived. This was a problem we knew how to fix! And so together we ended up ripping up the carpeting, sanding the floors, fixing up the kitchen—and scrubbing every surface until we could see our identical reflections in it. By the time Antoinette moved in, it was as good as new.

The first night Antoinette was going to spend in her own place, she realized she had forgotten to pack any spoons, so she walked back around the corner to her old apartment and took the elevator up to the sixth floor. She was about to turn her key in the door when she stopped, reminding herself, *I no longer live here.* She rang the bell. Kris opened the door and said, "Hey! What's up? Tricia's in the shower." And in that moment, all of Antoinette's sadness melted away. She finally knew in her heart—not just her head—that everything was going to be okay. It was the first time that Antoinette felt something like parental pride for Tricia that she'd taken this exciting new step, as she stood there and found herself thinking, *Oh, Trish, all grown up. It happens so fast!* Antoinette borrowed a couple spoons and walked back to her own apartment, and when she closed the door behind her she realized she hadn't even gotten to see Tricia during her quick visit. But she'd felt her.

We'd been each other's other half for so long, our bond had transcended the laws of physical time and space. Meaning, even when we weren't together, *we were together;* we were still each other's Aces, and we always would be, regardless of whether we lived in the same apartment or the same city or even the same state.

Our relationship has grown and changed in the years since, just as the two of us as individuals have grown and changed. That'll be true for you and your Ace, too. Things won't always stay the same— but if the bond is strong enough, it will always be there.

When we both went to bed that night, in our own homes, it felt exactly like the first night we'd spent in our first shared apartment on Gold Street. We knew that by taking this next big step—deciding to live apart, for the first time ever—we'd each put our faith in the other, our confidence in the other, just like always. Antoinette was embarking on her true independent journey, and Tricia was starting the next chapter with the love of her life. We'd pushed each other, challenged each other, and we were still in the big city together at the beginning of our next great adventure.

On the Download

Your Ace is another pair of eyes.
In the fast-paced, high-stakes world that is your life, you'll need someone to tell your stories to, to bounce ideas off of, and to help you put things in perspective. You'll want your Ace to help you see when you're doubting yourself, missing the point, or getting otherwise stonewalled by the Status Quo.

When you give confidence, you get confidence.
Build a relationship with an Ace by being an Ace—supplying confidence, straight talk, help, and compassion. When you put yourself out there as a source of strength for others, you'll find that others will give you support when you need it.

Be the person your Ace needs you to be.
When your Ace is in a bind or floundering, she needs you to help her break out of her brain rut, the hamster wheel, the spiral of self-doubt. Make room for her feelings, and then help her snap out of them.

Embrace the yin and yang.
Your Ace's strengths should complement your weaknesses, and your Ace's weaknesses should complement your strengths. The saying "Opposites attract" exists for a reason. You should seek out people who look, talk, and see the world in different ways.

Lighten the mood.
When your Ace is trapped in a spiral of self-doubt, and all the worries and negative thoughts are echoing endlessly inside her head, you need to break the spell by making your Ace laugh. When you laugh, you break the cycle of stale Status Quo thinking.

Grow and know when to let go.
You and your Ace should always be pushing each other to learn and grow. But not everyone grows at the same pace. Your relationship will change and evolve, just as you as individuals change and evolve. So know when it's time to let your Ace leave the nest. Even if you're not always around to counsel, console, and celebrate with each other, you'll still feel each other's presence.

chapter eight

Don't Just Be a Leader, Be a Boss Lady

n late April 2014 we took a trip to Jamaica, our ancestral homeland, when Carnival festivities were in their full and glorious swing; the beaches lit up at night looked like a mirror image of the constellations shining above us in the night sky, and the music sounded like it was being ferried inland on the back of a warm sea breeze. We went villa hopping, splashed around like giddy children in the pool, explored the jungles of Port Antonio, and watched the sun crest the horizon after an early-morning dance party. It was *so* necessary! Vacations are both the coffee and the champagne of the working life: they recharge you when you're spent, and nothing tastes better when you've really earned it.

We were having a lovely time, but Antoinette could tell that beneath the surface something was bothering Tricia—she couldn't quite seem to let loose and relax. At this point, Tricia and Kris had been married for seven happy years. They were soul mates. Kris had a sixth sense, always knowing what Tricia needed. They were the yin to the other's yang. Antoinette saw them as #couplegoals.

> **NETTE**
> What's going on? You good?

> **TRICIA**
> Who, me? I'm great.

Like many of us, Tricia has been known to downplay challenges and power through personal problems; she'd put up a cheerful front because she hated to burden or bother others with whatever was on her mind. Luckily Antoinette saw right through it. As we reclined on padded deck chairs on our hotel room's tiled balcony during a lull in the action one afternoon, Antoinette asked her again—what, really, was wrong?—and said she wouldn't take "nothing" for an answer.

Tricia sighed the sigh of a thousand sighs. She knew that once she said what she was about to say she would finally have to acknowledge it for what it was—the truth. Once she uttered it, there were no take-backs, no denials. There was no more cheerfully "powering through"; there was only dealing with the fallout.

> **TRICIA**
> There's something wrong with my marriage.
> It's not working right.

> **NETTE**
> I love you. Keep talking.

It took a lot of Antoinette's composure to play it cool in that moment, because there were about 1.5 million thoughts swirling around frantically in her mind, the first five being: *(1) WTF? (2) But Tricia and*

Kris always seem so happy together. (3) How could I have missed this? (4) WTF?
And then, *(5) Oh, no, Tricia must be really hurting inside.* But she kept her
face blank, not betraying her surprise, only broadcasting her concern.
She knew that what Tricia needed from her was empathy, not panic.

TRICIA

```
Something's just off, like the way you
just can't ever get totally comfortable
when there's even a little bit of beach
sand in your bedsheets. It wasn't always
like this. I just don't know if it's growing
pains or if we're growing apart. I know that
marriages change and evolve like everything
else, but it's as if somewhere along the
way we started going in the wrong direction
without knowing it. Now I worry we've gone
too far to turn back.
```

We talked nonstop for the next who-knows-how-many hours,
until the sun slid down the blue sky and hovered over the water,
shimmering like gold. We probed, we hypothesized, we looked at
every angle, trying to figure out what had gone wrong. There were
no glaring relationship problems like infidelity or fighting. Tricia
and Kris got along well! They were so connected. Yet they were
also disconnected. They knew each other inside and out. Yet they
seemed not always to know what the other one needed. Tricia knew
it wasn't only recent circumstances causing these issues, and yet recent circumstances seemed to have magnified them. The best way
she could describe it was that she and Kris didn't seem to be on the
same page—almost like they weren't even reading the same book.

Things did *look* good from the outside. Kris was generous and
demonstrative, but there were smaller absences. Sometimes, it just
didn't seem like he could or even wanted to show up for Tricia in
the basic way she needed. Take the surprise Narrative_ party that

Antoinette organized for Tricia six months after the company was off the ground. Tricia had been working long-ass hours to get it up and running, and Antoinette wanted to celebrate the accomplishment, so she rallied the crew, rented out Le Baron on the Lower East Side, and asked people to pitch in. Kris was super helpful and supportive, paying for some of the party expenses and getting his company to provide gift bag swag to all the partygoers. But the day of the party, Kris called Antoinette to say that his meeting in Charlotte was gonna run late so he didn't think he could get on a flight and make it to the party.

"Oh, you *need* to make it to this party," Antoinette said.

But he didn't. It was a small thing on its own, but it signaled the larger disconnect.

Now, sitting out on the balcony of the hotel, overlooking the waves cresting onto the empty, moonlit beach, Tricia didn't know if she had enabled him. Maybe she hadn't made her needs clear. Maybe this was her fault. Maybe she'd been spending too much time on work. Maybe she should've never started Narrative_.

Over the rest of the trip, Antoinette tried to get Tricia to open up when she could, and also to have fun to whatever extent she could. And by the time we came home, well rested and sun-soaked, Antoinette had convinced Tricia to talk to a therapist and get some expert advice.

Soon after, during a double session, her therapist, Boss Lady (and renowned psychologist and author) Esther Perel, told Tricia that she needed to articulate her thoughts to Kris. And that meant all of them: how her marriage felt stalled, how they'd grown apart, how difficult it was that he was always traveling and they never seemed to have time to talk about the relationship. If he's always traveling, Esther said, why not write him a letter he can read on a plane? At thirty-five thousand feet, there's plenty of time and space to read and think. Truth!

Tricia wrote him a letter, full of heart and soul, and slipped it into his carry-on bag on a Friday morning before he flew to Cleveland for work. Meanwhile, Tricia had her own work to worry about. Narrative_ was scheduled to deliver one of its biggest and most important pitches to date the following Monday. As in *the next* business day. And, well, they still didn't have it down. Not even close. So despite her dejected mood and her preoccupied mind, Tricia went in to work. She and her team stayed late, but even once they called it quits, the pitch still wasn't clean. Tricia told everyone the bad news: "We're gonna have to finish this over the weekend. Let's take tomorrow off, and we'll come in on Sunday to wrap it up. I know we got this. We can do this. We will do this."

The thing was: Tricia wasn't buying her own pep talk. She wasn't sure they *could* do this, that they *had* this, that it was *going* to get done. They had a lot to polish and perfect in time for Monday, and she happened to have some other things—like the future of her marriage— weighing on her mind.

That Sunday morning, Tricia was getting ready to head into the office when she heard the front door close. Kris was home. When she walked into the living room, he was sitting on the couch, and Tricia could tell he'd read the letter, thought about the letter, was thinking about the letter. But what did it all mean? She sat down next to him. Kris said he had read the letter, had thought about the letter, and was still thinking about the letter. He looked at her with sad eyes. "I agree with what you're saying. Something's not quite right."

It was now real—painfully real. Tricia had lived with these thoughts for months, and now they were out in the open. But she didn't have time to talk through, or even process, what had just happened. Her team was waiting for her, counting on her, back at the office. She hopped into a cab and sped uptown, she got into the elevator of her office building, and as the doors slowly closed, she let out a deep, sad sigh.

It was the longest elevator ride of her life.

Time dilated, contracted, stopped. Then it hit her like a right jab in her stomach: her marriage was over. They were both sad, they loved each other, but neither one of them was rushing to save the day. Neither one of them seemed to have the energy to save the day. And as the elevator lumbered slowly upward, the second floor turning into the third, then the fourth, Tricia realized that in a matter of seconds she needed to pull herself together and be someone else entirely.

What the moment required was not someone whose marriage had fallen apart. What the moment required was a leader, a Boss Lady—someone with confidence, compassion, and cool; someone other people believe in and trust. Tricia knew that the moment she was about to walk into would require as much strength as she could muster.

As the elevator doors opened, she wiped her cheeks, took a deep breath, and knew that when she opened the glass door to the Narrative_ office she needed to stride in there with her head high. She needed to be the fearless CEO her team—the people depending on her—needed her to be. **When your team needs you, you show up.** Because when you're a leader it's no longer about getting to the top. You are the top. Now you have to look out for all the people below.

Even as the pit in her stomach seemed to sink into her toes—*her marriage was over*—Tricia opened the glass door, saw her entire team look up at her, and took another deep breath. Here we go.

TRICIA
Ashley, let's review the strategic setup to make sure it supports the final creative. Aaron, we have three idea territories—let's

```
lock in top-line budgets—where are you with
them? Swang, let's get the final mocks locked.
When can I review? Ben, come by my office in
ten minutes for a creative review. We need to
tighten up two of the territories. Today is
the first and last day. Let's make magic!
```

And with that, the team got to work. Tricia walked into her office, setting her bags down and, with them, all her problems. The personal shit could wait—it had to. Anyway, she couldn't do anything about her marriage in that moment. What she could do was be a Boss Lady.

What mattered right then was that she be in control of only and exactly *what she could control*—and that was killing it. Boss Ladies are always killing it—and Tricia knew she needed to embody that role: to dial in, inhabit, occupy. And so she did.

Tricia went over the strategic setup with Ashley, encouraging her to follow her instincts to identify the target audience and understand their motivations. She ran the numbers with Aaron, and together they were able to cut development costs and get the budget within range. Swang's mockups were tight, so they spent some time perfecting the typography and placement to make sure all the essential details popped. The meeting with Ben took longer than ten minutes, but they managed to figure out those territories in under twenty.

Time flew. Coffee was made and drunk. Shadows lengthened. The sun sank. More coffee was made and drunk. The stars came out. Then the moon—and the day was over. Tricia was the last one to leave the building at 10 p.m.—but the job was done, and they'd done it well. Really well. Everyone was proud of what they'd pulled off. As she waited for a cab, Tricia was the proudest of all: not only because her team had killed it, but also because she had been able to keep her composure despite everything that was going on. She'd put her emotions aside, rolled up her sleeves, and pushed her team—and herself—to do their best work. She did what Boss Ladies do. She put the team first.

The Status Quo would have you believe that a Boss Lady is someone with a fancy job title, an expense account, and a swank office. Not so. A Boss Lady may eventually obtain those things, but they don't define her. What defines you as a Boss Lady has nothing to do with the number of zeros on your paycheck or how many people report to you. It's the ability to rise above the noise and get things done, to bring out the best in others, to instill confidence, and to give back to your team—in a big way.

Now, headed south on Seventh Avenue, Tricia didn't know what was going to happen with Kris, but whatever it was, she knew she was ready to face it. It wasn't going to be easy. But nothing great is. Tricia returned home that night with more confidence than she'd begun the day with.

That's when she knew for sure that when shit hits the fan your inner Boss Lady will remind you what you're capable of. Your Boss Lady essence will prop you up.

Leading Is Believing

We've always seen synergy between how we work and how we live. We bring the same kind of passion and commitment to our friendships that we do to our work, and we deliver the same kind of intensity and loyalty at work that we do when we're kicking it with friends. We see the skills in one area carrying over into the other. We believe that if you have what it takes to lead in life, then you have what it takes to lead at work. That's why the final chapter of this book is about how to emerge as a Boss Lady with your crew, and in your career.

First as a salesperson and then as cofounder and CEO of

Narrative_, Tricia learned how to become a general; she learned to plan, strategize, and coordinate. She knew that to beat the Status Quo you need to make sure all your troops are ready, willing, and able. You need to innovate new ideas—those are your tactical advantage. And you need to know your market—that's the battlefield.

You need to be creative, strategic, and inspiring; you need to deliver.

First as a producer and then as a VP of branded entertainment, Antoinette learned how to become more like an orchestra conductor. When you're producing a TV show, everything has to sync up and harmonize. You need to make sure all your segments are in order and ready to go. There's the show—it needs creative control. There's talent—the host or guest needs to feel taken care of. Then there's the Network—you have to deliver the rating and creative innovation so brands are willing to pay top dollar.

You need to be responsive, perceptive, and organized; you need to know everyone's part cold.

And we both apply these same skills to our crew, just as we do to our work.

As soon as our friend Nicole told us she was pregnant, for example, Tricia sprang into action. Her first move was to hit #1 on speed dial.

> **TRISH**
> Oh, we're *going* to do a baby shower.
> Yo—this is the first meeting of the Baby
> Shower Committee.

> **NETTE**
> Right here, right now. Let's get rolling.

We got to work, putting together a write-up, making mood boards on Pinterest, picking out supplies from Party City and Amazon. We got a bunch of Polaroid cameras to create instant keepsakes and selected floral arrangements. Then we sent the plan to another friend of Nicole's, who manages events at ESPN. "You guys are on steroids," she said. "This is insane. You figured everything out."

That's how we roll; always have. Because it doesn't matter how much is on your plate: **you gotta go all-in on the things that matter**. If someone in your crew is counting on you, you show up—with intensity. As if it was your job. And trust us, the payoff is always there. In this case, the baby shower was a smash hit, and Nicole was moved to tears because she felt so lucky to have friends to support her down this new path in her life.

Some people think that to seem "professional" you have to show up as some alternate version of yourself in the workplace. But remember from chapter 5: you can't be your best self if you're always trying to be someone else. And you are still the same *you* at work as you are when you're off the clock. Both with your crew and at work, you need to believe in yourself, go all-in on everything that matters to you, and inspire others to do the same.

Our girl and Boss Lady Ayesha Curry thinks a lot about how passion for your people and profession can be intertwined, and she knows a thing or two about being a Boss Lady both at home and at work. The author-chef, entrepreneur, mother of three, and actress told us: "My work and my passions are always focused around family and food. My philosophy has always been that relationships are built at home and around the family table. So everything I do tries to entice togetherness. Togetherness is the key. This is truly what drives me." At the core of what Ayesha does in her personal and professional life is create opportunities for people to connect and belong. Ayesha's superpower is bringing people together, to inspire each other to become the best versions of themselves.

Our OG Boss Lady

The first true Boss Lady we ever saw in action was Grandma. Grandma didn't go to college—or even finish high school—and she never became a VP or CEO of a company. But she is the reason we did. She was the fiercest Boss Lady we ever knew. If it weren't for the skills she imparted to us and the spirit of perseverance and passion that she modeled for us, we don't know where we'd be today. Grandma was a **Fearless Optimist.** She never gave up. And she never stopped believing in possibility. Or in us.

Grandma was our biggest fan. She thought we were the most amazing little things on Planet Earth, and so she made us feel like superheroes. "Well, what do you mean you're not going to try out for the spelling bee? You're so smart," she told Antoinette. Grandma always believed that we could do anything we set our minds to, and that belief fueled our sense of confidence from an early age. Perhaps because she'd pulled off the impossible with her own life: every single one of her eight kids grew up to have a better life than she had.

She always made us feel special—but with specialness came great responsibility. She reminded us of our culture and our obligations, like the fact that the family had come here so that all of us could have more opportunity. She gave us unconditional love, but not free passes. She never needed to tell us "No" twice; we heard her the first time. Plus, we didn't ever want to make her mad, because we knew that she could curse down the place. Grandma was as sweet as the coconut drops we used to eat up, but she also dropped *F bombs* and *bumbaclots* like a truck driver.

When we were growing up, Mom had two full-time jobs—her actual job and us—so we spent a lot of time with Grandma. We used to love to walk around the neighborhood with her because she told us stories and always made even the most mundane sights seem exciting. One time when we were eight or nine, we were out on one of our adventures and heard footsteps close behind us. Suddenly, a teenage boy ripped Grandma's purse out of her hands, tucked it under his arm like a running back, and started sprinting up the street. We were so scared and startled, we just froze like a pair of snowmen. But not Grandma. She danced out of her shoes and sprinted up the block after the little hooligan. "Come back here with my fucking bag!" she yelled. "Drop mi bag or you'll be one sorry bumbohole!"

As we said, she was fearless; nothing could shake her.

That was true even as she got older and on into her seventies. When we were home for Christmas during our sophomore year at Skidmore, she insisted on taking us to the drugstore to buy us all the supplies we'd need for the next semester. We rolled our eyes, but we knew there was no use arguing—not with Grandma. It was cold and snowy that winter, and when we got to the drugstore Grandma slipped on some black ice and went down hard. We rushed to her side. Her forehead was bleeding, and it looked like she'd also sprained her ankle (turned out she broke it!). We hoisted her into the back of the car and drove back to Mom's. We showed up at the door with Grandma propped up in between us, like an injured football player being helped off the field by two teammates. "Why are you back here, and what the hell did you do to Grandma?" Mom asked.

So then we all went to the ER, and at about 2 a.m. Grandma got released with six stitches in her head. As we walked back to the car, she asked, "So, you think the drugstore is still open or what?"

That was just like Grandma. She was tough.

She embodied that fearless spirit through her seventies, then her eighties, and into her nineties. But eventually age caught up to her, as it will for all of us. When Grandma passed away in 2017, we felt a profound loss. When someone has been so potent, so powerful, so present in your life, it's hard to wrap your head around the fact that they are gone. But she was a true Boss Lady till the end. She left a lump sum of money to be used for her funeral, and even left instructions—they were specific as hell—about how she wanted the service to go! Leave it to Grandma to plan her own funeral, we chuckled to ourselves.

We wake up every morning determined to carry on the Boss Lady legacy that we learned from Grandma: to constantly channel her energy, intensity, and optimism. She knew that to make your way in life, you need **to be the person you need yourself to be.** Grandma may never have sat down at a blackjack table in her life, but she knew the art of the Double Down.

Boss Ladies of the World Unite

We grew up with Pat Benatar spinning on the turntable, belting out tunes while Mom got her groove on cleaning the house. Even as kids, we sensed she was something of a kindred spirit: a no-fucks-given rock 'n' roll goddess who wrote and performed songs like "Hit Me with Your Best Shot," "We Belong," and "Invincible."

In 2015, *USA Today* published a profile of Tricia and the Virtual Reality campaign she'd launched for Under Armour (it was just about the best lede ever written: "The sign on Tricia Clarke-Stone's desk says it all: Boss Lady." Truth!). A day later, Tricia got a voicemail notification on e-mail. The subject heading was: VOICEMAIL FROM PAT BENATAR.

Naturally, she almost lost her shit when she saw it. Pat Benatar! *On her voicemail.* Was this even real? Was she being punked?

Turned out that Pat had seen the profile and thought that Tricia was "doing things that were different and important," so she decided to reach out. Game recognizes game, and Pat had sensed it immediately in Tricia.

Tricia and Pat connected and established a rapport: they both hoped they could someday find something to collaborate on. A year or so later, when Tricia was in L.A. on business, she texted Pat, saying that she was in town and had some time to kill. Pat said, "Come out to Malibu."

When Pat Benatar tells you to come out to Malibu, you put the top down, take the 10 to the 1, and pull up to her sprawling beachfront property as quick as you can. Lunch was served, and as they chatted the conversation inevitably turned to the recent election, Trump, and the upcoming Women's March in D.C., which Pat couldn't attend because of a show she was headlining in the Caribbean. She was bummed out to miss what promised to be a watershed moment, which prompted Tricia to ask:

> **TRICIA**
> Well, what can we do to show everyone that
> even if every woman can't be standing there,
> at least all women are standing together?

> **PAT BENATAR**
> I'm game for anything you can think up.

Tricia thought two thoughts in one second. Her first thought was: *I'm having a light lunch on a veranda overlooking the Pacific Ocean with Pat fucking Benatar. Damn!* And her second thought was: *What's Pat Benatar known for? Being a pioneering badass Boss Lady who rocks as hard as she rolls. She needs to do a song!*

> **TRICIA**
> You need to do a song. You need to do a song
> we can share with the world.

Pat's eyes lit up like candles on Christmas Eve! By the end of the lunch, Pat promised Tricia she'd think about a song and a collaborator and get back to her.

Two days later, when Tricia was back in New York, her phone rang.

> **PAT BENATAR**
> After you left, I called Linda Perry. She has a song for us. I just recorded the demo. I'm sending it to you now.

This time, Tricia had three thoughts at once. The first was: *Linda Perry—as in the OG badass Boss Lady and songwriter who's written for Christina Aguilera, Pink, Adele, and Alicia Keys, and who founded two of her own labels?* The second was: *Shit, I promised Pat Benatar I would help her share her song with the world!* The third was: *If I'm going to kill this, I need to get to work.*

Tricia listened to the song, "Shine"—and shit was lit!

Tricia immediately called her Ace and gave her the breakdown. "We'll need a website and something that'll get eyeballs," Antoinette said. "I'll write copy. Over and out." Then Antoinette picked up the phone and activated her crew—while Tricia gave the breakdown to the Narrative_ team. They brainstormed until the clouds parted and a ray of light shone through.

The developer built the website; it took him two or three nights to knock it out. The art director designed a logo. Tricia's right hand, Aaron, helped to project-manage and researched what charity they should give all the proceeds to. Antoinette worked her old production game and pitched the story—Pat Benatar creating a single for the Women's March—to all her EP friends at the daytime shows. And both of us hit up all the rest of our tribe—Jen, Nicole, Latham, Talitha, Constance, Chenoa, Deirdre—to post on social.

Tricia worked with her team at Narrative_ to come up with a meme generator that would allow users to upload a picture of a woman who inspired them to shine and type in a few words about why. A few days before the Women's March, #ShineTogether went live. Thousands upon thousands of women of all races, ethnicities, and backgrounds used the meme generator to express their gratitude to the Boss Ladies who had made a difference in their own lives.

We decided to price downloads of the song at sixty-nine cents, as opposed to ninety-nine, to raise awareness about the gender wage gap. And we decided that any and all proceeds would go to the BA Rudolph Foundation, which supports women pursuing careers in government, politics, and public policy.

Finally, the big day came. The Women's March in New York City was the first time we'd ever marched for anything (we're still learning!), and it felt incredible to be part of that moment in time. All those women coming together, the energy, the camaraderie, the signs—the power was palpable. It was like a massive, marching (one could say shining) beacon of light.

This is what happens when Boss Ladies get together to make shit happen. Because when Boss Ladies join forces and combine their powers, they can do just about anything. That's the power that Boss Ladies have with one another: they inspire us to exponentially up our game. They support us. Ask much of us. Trust us. They push us to be our finest selves: fierce, focused, and fearless. Never give up, and never stop believing: that's the centrality of being a Boss Lady. **You are a Boss Lady.**

Remember: *Boss Lady* is a mode of being—irreducible, elemental. It doesn't matter where you work, what you do, or how much money you bank: we know you have this essence inside you. We know because of how you show grace under pressure instead of getting crushed by it. You breathe in through the nose, out from the mouth.

You make decisions, not problems. You *command*, you don't demand. You don't promise, you deliver. You *inspire*, you don't dictate. You *answer*, you don't prevaricate. You push us to be our own best selves, not low-res versions of someone else. You press play, not repeat. You never show fear. But you feel fear, sometimes, because you just know that fear is raw power to be refined into energy. You use that energy to power yourself—onward and upward in the direction of your dreams.

The future belongs to you, Boss Lady. We're counting on you. We believe in you. We've got your back. We'll never give up, and we'll never let you down.

Now, what are you waiting for?

Get out there, Boss Lady. The world needs you.

On the Download

When your team needs you, put your team first.
When you're a leader, it's no longer about getting to the top. You are the top. Now you have to look out for all the people below you. They look to you for answers, confidence, and support. That's a sacred bond, and Boss Ladies uphold it.

You gotta go all-in on the things that matter.
When you're engaged in any pursuit of importance—and we recommend you take on only pursuits that fall into this category—you must marshal all your strengths. What sets Boss Ladies apart is their ability to go all-in while others are still calculating.

Be a Fearless Optimist.
The most powerful force in the world is unflappable optimism. We all feel fear, but Boss Ladies broadcast fearlessness. No matter what the world throws at them, they remain unshakable.

Never give up, and don't stop believing.
Once you're a Boss Lady, these are the nonnegotiables. When you know that others are counting on you, it's impossible to give up.

Be the person you need yourself to be.
You'll never lead yourself astray if you keep asking yourself what you need, and you keep providing it for yourself. Don't wait like you're wounded; pounce like a panther to get what you seek.

You are a Boss Lady.
You are a leader. You are a fighter. And you inspire. There's no stopping you, and there's no telling what you can do with your superpowers. We believe in you.

BOSS LADY SOURCES

chapter one

"I was sort of a weirdo": Patricia Garcia, "Meet Lena Waithe, *Master of None*'s Wisest and Funniest BFF," *Vogue,* November 17, 2015, https://www.vogue.com/article/lena-waithe-denise-master-of-none.

"I see each and every one of you": Jess Cohen, *"Master of None*'s Lena Waithe Becomes First Black Woman to Win Emmy Award for Best Comedy Writing & Shouts Out LGBTQIA Community," E! Online, September 17, 2017, https://www.eonline.com/news/880897/masters-of-none-s-lena-waithe-becomes-first-black-woman-to-win-emmy-award-for-best-comedy-writing.

"I had never been around": Tre'vell Anderson, "With *Girls Trip* and a comedy special, Tiffany Haddish's 'calling card' is open for the taking," *LA Times,* July 20, 2017, https://www.latimes.com/entertainment/la-ca-black-women-comedy-tiffany-haddish-20170720-htmlstory.html.

"*They're just regular people*": Emma Brown, "In the Middle of Somewhere with Ava DuVernay and Emayatzy Corinealdi," *Interview* magazine,

October 9, 2012, https://www.interviewmagazine.com/film/ava-duvernay
-emayatzy-corinealdi.

"I love being underestimated,": Lynn Hirschberg, "Banksable," *New York
Times Magazine,* June 1, 2008, https://www.nytimes.com/2008/06/01/
magazine/01tyra-t.html.

chapter two

"I launched around the same time": Tyler McCall, "A Decade in Digital:
Leandra Medine Wants 'Man Repeller' to Outlive Her," Fashionista,
August 7, 2017, https://fashionista.com/2017/08/man-repeller-leandra
-medine-interview.

"The existing health care system": Stinson Carter, "A Day in the Life of
Anne Wojcicki," *WSJ. Magazine,* January 12, 2016, https://www.wsj.com/
articles/a-day-in-the-life-of-anne-wojcicki-1452613783.

"Michelle and I came": Interview with TAC.

chapter three

"Lists to me are everything": Interview with TAC.

"The journey will not be easy": Competitor.com, August 12, 2016,
https://www.youtube.com/watch?v=14BZb4xUvwI.

"Many people told me": https://leanin.org/stories/ursula-burns; Adam
Bryant, "Xerox's New Chief Tries to Redefine Its Culture," February 20,
2010, https://www.nytimes.com/2010/02/21/business/21xerox.html.

chapter four

"Don't listen to the so-called experts": http://joanjettbadrep.com/
Interviews/2000/weekender.shtml.

"Twenty-six years ago": Interview with TAC.

"I loved my pediatrician": Interview with TAC.

chapter six

"a downright boss in finance": Interview with TAC. Background: Declan Eytan,"How Model Grace Mahary Is Bringing Renewable Energy to Impoverished Communities Across Africa," August 28, 2017, https://www .forbes.com/sites/declaneytan/2017/08/28/how-model-grace-mahary-is -bringing-renewable-energy-to-impoverished-communities-across-africa/ #25ba70673ed0.

"Jennifer, Alicia, and Eva": Interview with TAC.

chapter seven

"I'm able to believe in myself": Interview with TAC.

chapter eight

"My work and my passions": Interview with TAC.

ACKNOWLEDGMENTS

This book was our baby, and it took a village. The wisdom we share in it, the stories that constitute it, and the energy behind it would not have been possible without the support and encouragement of Mom, aka the Swiss Army Knife, Audrey Clarke, as well as the rest of the clan—Aunt Norma, Aunt Monica, Aunt Leonie, and cousins Michelle, Tracey, Ian, Helena, and our little bro, Ernel. You all inspired us with your hard-won knowledge and your fierce love. And to Kris: you've always been so good to us, and an amazing partner to Tricia. And to Bryce: thanks for your lessons, support, and love.

Likewise, our through-thick-and-thin, ride-or-die Tribe has always shown us that no woman is an island and that we are all stronger together. Our world is better, fuller, and brighter because of you. For being with us on our journeys and supporting them, thank you Jen, Talitha, Tai, Nicole, Chenoa, Deirdre, Heather, Simone, Michelle, Constance, Nikki, Lori, Debbie, James, Tania, Emil, Kris,

Bryce, Damon, Cordell, Gary, Felicia, Marc, Russell Simmons, Jaha, Deb, and Pat Benatar.

To our Work Squads—CBS TV Network and WP Narrative_. You all make us want to do our best work.

To all the Boss Ladies who helped to make this book possible by taking the time to speak with us about their superpowers and superior skills—Grace Mahary, Ayesha Curry, Lacy Phillips, Ali Kriegsman and Alana Branston, Loren Ridinger, Anne Wojcicki, Carly Cushnie. Thanks also to the Boss Ladies who inspired us from afar—Ava DuVernay, Lena Waithe, Tyra Banks, Tiffany Haddish, Joan Jett, Leandra Medine Cohen, Ursula Burns, and Tori Bowie.

Thank you to everyone at Random House and at Currency for believing in our book and our hopes. We are so glad and grateful to have worked with the inimitable Talia Krohn as an editor—words cannot express our gratitude for your invaluable expertise and time in working with us on the manuscript. Your enthusiasm and intelligence are infectious. Thanks also to Tina Constable, Campbell Wharton, Nicole McArdle, and Stephen Boriack.

Thank you to our literary agent at Massie & McQuilkin and collaborator Elias Altman. E, not only was your belief in us at the beginning essential, but your keen and poetic insights helped us bring our stories to life. You truly get us and our vision—that's all and everything we could ask for. Thanks also to everyone at ACM for your support and hard work.

And thank you to all the young soon-to-be Boss Ladies, individuals we have had the opportunity to lead, be led by, or watch their leadership from afar, we want to say thank you for being an inspiration.

INDEX

ABOUT THE AUTHORS

Antoinette Clarke is a two-time Emmy Award–winning television producer and the VP of Branded Entertainment and Media Innovation at CBS Television Network. She is responsible for ideation, pitching, selling, negotiating, developing, and activating strategic branded content and advertiser partnerships across multiple platforms for the CBS Daytime slate of shows and specials.

In the previous decade, Antoinette worked as a producer for a variety of award-winning talk shows with hosts Montel Williams, Tyra Banks, Rachael Ray, and Nate Berkus. Throughout her career, Antoinette's contributions to producing hundreds of lifestyle-based shows—including social experiments, celebrity interviews, home and personal makeovers, holiday extravaganzas, and tentpole events—have led to some of the highest-rated episodes on daytime television. Years prior, she worked as the director of broadcast sales integration for Martha Stewart, where she collaborated with marketing and production teams, executed creative concepts, and managed integration sales activities.

A graduate of Skidmore College, Antoinette was honored with a Black Women in Media Award in 2017 and was 1 of 39 featured in *Adweek*'s annual Disruptors list in 2018.

Tricia Clarke-Stone is the cofounder and CEO of WP Narrative_, an award-winning creative and technology agency that was acquired by Hollywood producer Will Packer in 2017. Tricia founded Narrative_ with Russell Simmons in 2013, creating a new marketing agency model uniting code and culture. Known for being a boundary-pusher with a uniquely attuned business and creative mind, Tricia redefined the status quo with a mandate to future-proof brands, drive innovation, create transformative IP, and develop products and game-changing campaigns for start-ups and some of the world's most iconic brands.

Years prior, Tricia was the copresident of Global Grind, where she relaunched the media company, grew revenue by 500 percent, and created more than 100 cross-cultural, digital, social, and experiential campaigns for brands including Toyota, Pepsi, P&G, and AT&T. Emmis Communications was the first business to transform under Tricia's leadership; she built the company's first digital division, pioneered new concepts to drive growth and innovation, diversified revenue, and guided agencies and blue-chip brands to create cross-platform campaigns.

A graduate of Skidmore College, Tricia has been recognized for visionary tactics, earning spots on both *Ad Age*'s and *Crain's New York*'s 40 Under 40 lists, *Adweek*'s Disruptors, and Refinery29's Black Is the New Black, as well as numerous speaking engagements discussing the role of marketing in tech, entertainment, fashion, culture, and retail. She has been profiled in *The New York Times, Fast Company, Elle, USA Today, Marie Claire, Forbes,* and *Fortune.*

Antoinette and Tricia are identical twins.